# IN YOUR NATURE

James T. Colbert

HOG PRESS

Hog Press
an imprint of Culicidae Press®
PO Box 5069
Madison, WI 53705-5069
hogpress.com
editor@hogpress.com

Hog Press

IN YOUR NATURE
Copyright © 2025 by James T. Colbert
All rights reserved.

No part of this book may be reproduced in any form by any electronic or mechanized means (including photocopying, recording, or information storage and retrieval) without written permission, except in the case of brief quotations embodied in critical articles and reviews. For more information, please visit culicidaepress.com

ISBN: 978-1-68315-142-5

Our books may be purchased in bulk for promotional, educational or business use. Please contact your local bookseller or the Culicidae Press Sales Department at +1-352-215-7558 or by email at sales@culicidaepress.com

culicidaepress.bsky.social – facebook.com/culicidaepress
threads.net/@culicidaepress – instagram.com/culicidaepress
x.com/culicidaepress

Design by polytekton © 2025

This book is dedicated to my children and grandchildren. My hope is that they will live in a world with amazing biological diversity for many years to come.

# Table of Contents

Foreword — 5

Newbie — 9
The Bridge — 15
Bugs and Snakes — 21
Fishing — 27
Mountain Men — 35
Ice and Fire — 45
Upland Birds — 51
Mushrooms — 59
The Navy — 65
The Lichen in Winter — 73
Downstream — 85
Liquid Water — 91
Peak Experience — 99
More Fishing — 105
Happy Animals — 111
Ducks — 119
What's in Your Nature? — 127

Acknowledgments — 134

# Foreword

*I will argue that every scrap of biological diversity is priceless, to be learned and cherished, and never to be surrendered without a struggle.*

E.O. Wilson

I was born and raised in Cedar Rapids, Iowa. I grew up in a 'blue-collar' family with two parents, four siblings, and one dog. I was a rather undistinguished student in the parochial schools I attended. My father insisted that I go to college anyway. The environment I encountered, first at the University of Northern Iowa and then at Iowa State University, freed from the strictures of Catholicism, changed my life. I went on to study plant biology in graduate school at the University of Wisconsin-Madison. After earning my Ph.D., I was fortunate enough to have a career as a faculty member at Colorado State University (three years) and Iowa State University (thirty-three years). I was both a researcher and a teacher, but my true passion was helping students learn about the amazing biological world that we are all a part of. Some of the earliest, and most important, 'students' I had were the son and daughter that my wife and I produced together.

The stories that follow are all true, though some aspects of the timing and order of events were modified to make the telling of the stories easier. Memory, of course, is imperfect and some events may not have occurred quite the way related here. I write about these events not because my life is especially interesting, or unique in any important way, but because, according to my wife, I'm a 'compulsive sharer'. My hope is that relating these stories will encourage others to notice and learn about the wonders of their local biological world as they go through life. 'Meeting the neighbors' so to speak. Biology is everywhere, not just in exotic locales somewhere else in the world. Hopefully, the more people learn, the more of that knowledge they will share with other people in their life.

Yes, I included scientific names. This was not pretentiousness or an attempt to annoy potential readers. I was seeking to be unambiguous. Suppose that I mention a plant that I call 'cocklebur' (I do — in the chapter titled 'Ducks'). You might be familiar with a plant species called 'noogoora bur' and assume I'm talking about a different plant species. Or you might be familiar with 'rough cocklebur', 'clotbur', 'large cocklebur', 'woolgarie bur', or 'heartleaf cocklebur' and make the same assumption. As it turns out, all of these 'common names' refer to the very same species: *Xanthium strumarium*. Feel free to completely ignore the scientific names, but if you wish to learn more about any of these species, the scientific name is an excellent starting point.

> *Memory is a complicated thing, a relative to truth, but not its twin.*
>
> Barbara Kingsolver

# Newbie

*While we are born with curiosity and wonder and our early years full of the adventure they bring, I know such inherent joys are often lost.*

Sigurd Olson

It was the spring I turned five. We lived in an old farmhouse at the edge of a small town. The back of our yard bordered a place owned by an older couple. They had a chicken (*Gallus gallus*) coop. The inside of the coop was tall enough to walk through, warm, and smelling of damp feathers. Sometimes they would let me go in and carefully pick up eggs and place them into a bucket filled with straw. I think they would give my mother a few of the eggs to take home and help feed her young family.

On a hot sunny day later that summer I was outside by myself. My three sisters were too young to be outside by themselves, and my mother was busy inside. Our long side yard was dominated by a big tree, that I now realize was a white pine (*Pinus strobus*). All along, and extending far beyond, our side yard was a corn (*Zea mays*) field. The corn was tall, full height in late summer, but still dark green. In between our yard and the corn field was a dense row of small trees. In hindsight I recognize them as white cedars (*Thuja occidentalis*). They had multiple stems, interwoven branches, and dense foliage. I had been told to stay well away from the corn field. Little kids could wander into the corn and never be found, I had been informed. It was very hot in the full Sun in our yard and the shade under the cedars looked inviting. I wasn't sure whether the cedars counted as part of the corn field or not.

With considerable trepidation I passed the border between our brightly lit mowed grass and the cool shade beneath the cedars. I could see the corn, but it seemed far enough away to still be safe. I turned to my left, and I could see patches of our yard through the branches on my left and dimly visible corn plants on my right. From this perspective I could not tell how far the cedars extended in front of me. Slowly, I started walking through the trees. It was shady and cool, and it smelled nice. I tripped over a low branch and stumbled toward the corn field. I caught my balance on the trunk of a bigger cedar. The corn looked a bit close, and I corrected my course accordingly. I kept walking, glancing frequently to my left to be sure I could still catch glimpses of the safety of our yard, and to my right to be sure the corn hadn't gotten closer. It seemed that I had gone quite a way, and I started to turn around hoping I'd be able to find my way back, but it was all starting to look the same. I wasn't sure what to do. I stopped. I couldn't see the end of the trees and I was scared to go any farther. I knew I couldn't go right – the corn field was there. I decided to go to my left. Within just a few steps the Sun blazed, and I could see the big white pine standing tall in our side yard. I breathed a sigh of relief and ran through the side yard to the back door of our house. Sometime later that summer the sky grew dark well before sundown. The wind began to blow. Thunder boomed and lightning flashed. Rain began to hammer the roof of our house. The wind rose and began to roar. Mom and dad took us into the basement, probably telling us that all would be ok. It was ok – for us. But the next morning revealed that the big white pine had been toppled over with its roots now exposed to the bright light of day.

Summer was coming to an end, and the corn plants were beginning to turn tan. It must have been a Saturday because my dad was home. He asked me if I would like to go fishing. I'm pretty sure I didn't know what fishing was, but I was happy to go with my dad. My dad brought a fishing pole. We got in our car, an old station wagon and drove somewhere. We walked down a steep bank to a pond with brown water, rippling in a light breeze and sending reflections in all directions. The pole had a bait casting reel and black fishing line. My dad dug in the ground and found a few worms that went into an empty soup can. Next, he went back up the bank to the edge of a corn field and found a couple of dry last year's corn cobs. A small piece of corn cob was tied to the fishing line above the sinker, while the hook dangled below the sinker. My dad threaded a worm onto the hook and casted the line out into the water. He told me to watch the dark corn cob piece floating on the surface of the dark water. I watched. It was warm and sunny, but we were in the shade of a tall tree and there was a breeze. The air felt cool and smelled of pond. I saw a frog crouched near the bank. I forgot all about watching the corn cob. My dad said something loudly, re-capturing my attention, and he started to reel in line. As the line got closer to the shallows a small fish appeared struggling against the pull of the line. It seemed as though my dad had performed a magic trick. There was a small bullhead (*Ameiurus nebulosus*) flopping on the bank. My dad put the fish on a stringer, tied the stringer to a branch, and tossed the fish into the shallows. He put more bait on the hook and casted out again. My eyes strained to remain focused on the corn cob floating in the water. This time, I saw the corn cob move, first one way then the other. And then – it disappeared under the surface. My dad raised the tip of the pole to hook the fish and handed me the pole, showing me which way to turn the crank. I reeled, amazed at how hard the fish pulled back. I kept reeling and the fish, a small bluegill (*Lepomis macrochirus*), slid flopping onto the shore. I watched in a state of excited amazement as my dad unhooked the fish and added it to our stringer. I was hooked too. We caught one more small-sized bullhead before heading back home to clean our catch and fry up some fish. I remember the salty, crunchy, taste of the fish my mom put on my plate as she pulled the meat away from the bones. Somewhere there is a picture of me holding up that stringer of small fish in the driveway of our house – the opposite side from the blown over pine tree. I haven't seen that picture for a long time, but I still get excited every time I catch a fish.

Many years later I was fortunate enough to relive the 'first fish' experience with both of my children, and subsequently, with my grandson and my two granddaughters. Smiling as I watched the confused look as they tried to figure out how to work the fishing reel while the fish pulled on the line. Listening to their squeals of delight. Their eyes wide with wonder as the fish was landed, shining, and flopping, in the sunshine. Hesitant fingers touching the cool slippery surface of the fish's body. And, later, the young, slender, fingers of my granddaughters breaded fillets in preparation for a fish fry. I had become part of a long tradition amongst humans (*Homo sapiens*), teaching the next generations how to accomplish the 'magic trick' of pulling dinner out of a body of water.

# The Bridge

*Wilderness is not a luxury but a necessity of the human spirit.*

Edward Abbey

My family had moved to the 'big city' a couple years prior. A new, bigger, house as well as some new friends. Second grade was over. We were released to the wild for the summer. My friend and I were walking home in the bright sunshine of an early summer afternoon. Endless possibilities seemed to stretch out before us. Third grade seemed impossibly far in the future. Parenting was different in those days. When kids were not in school, they were pretty much released on their own recognizance. With rare, and sometimes tragic, exceptions it was not a problem for the parents or the kids. There was an implied understanding that the kids would be within shouting distance around lunch time and dinner time and be back inside before dark. Growling stomachs encouraged compliance.

Some days later as endless time on the playground began to feel a bit stale a novel plan arose. How about taking a walk somewhere? Near the end of the school year my friend and I had both been part of a group of Cub Scouts given the extra special opportunity to be present at the ribbon cutting ceremony for a new bridge over a local creek, featuring the mayor himself wielding the scissors. It seemed like that might be a good destination. I have no memory of asking our mothers for permission. If we did, it would not surprise me if they said "Ok – but be back in time for dinner." They also might have said "stay out of the water," demonstrating parental due diligence. We were eight. Different times.

We started walking south down a street that crossed the street our homes were on, just one house apart from each other. We didn't know which way 'south' was then, but I do now. We took nothing but our clothes and shoes. No water. No food. No coat in case the warm summer afternoon worked up to a thunderstorm. We walked on the sidewalk, looking carefully for cars as we crossed each east-west street. Slowly the number of houses began to decrease until we passed a last house that was set back from the street a bit. It clearly had needed a new coat of paint decades ago and some of the windows were broken. Keeping a careful watch on the overgrown yard we walked past as quickly as our short legs would allow. We could now see down a long, gentle, slope to a thin line of trees in the distance. We continued along the road down the hill. The sidewalk ended and we walked along between the edge of the road and the corn fields.

I don't remember being thirsty, but I probably was. It was warm and, as I later learned, it was just over a mile from my house to the bridge over the creek. But – here we were at the bridge over the creek. We had waited for a long, and fast, freight train that crossed the road on our way to the bridge. Loud and more than a little scary. Now we were looking over the bridge railing at the roiling brown water rapidly flowing under the bridge. We entertained ourselves for a while by throwing rocks at logs and at patches of tan foam floating with the current. We decided to walk down into the woods upstream of the bridge, while both telling each other to 'stay out of the water'. We pushed through a thick stand of abrasive-stemmed giant ragweed (*Ambrosia trifida*) and entered the edge of the woods. The Sun's light was dimmed by the layers of leaves above us. The riparian deciduous forest with silver maple (*Acer saccharinum*), box elder (*Acer negundo*), river birch, (*Betula nigra*), and cottonwood (*Populus deltoides*), quickly hid any evidence of both the bridge and road leading to it. We were still pretty sure that we knew how to get back to the road.

We wandered around through the patchwork of bright light and shade in the woods slowly getting closer to the bank of the creek. We had to cross a puddle left from when the creek had been even higher. Our shoes got muddy, but we agreed that we weren't really getting in the water. We made it to a little opening along the bank. There was water flowing right past us and we were definitely not getting in. But, of course, that did not stop us from throwing things in. A large number of sticks, which floated nicely, and clods of earth, which didn't float at all, were added to the muddy waters of the creek.

Of course, even the best of times must come to an end, and our stomachs may have been starting to growl. We decided to head back and even remembered which direction the road was. And then we saw it. A turtle. Walking slowly on land through the woods. It had a high humped shell. We looked at it as it looked at us. We poked it a little with a stick and it withdrew entirely into its shell. We picked it up for closer inspection — it was remarkably heavy — and then set it back down. Slowly its head and legs reemerged, and it proceeded to continue on its slow way out of our young lives. We watched it a while longer, but growling stomachs have their own sense of time. Needless to say, we arrived back at our respective homes, probably thirsty, hungry and tired, but no worse for the wear.

Even at eight, I knew it was a 'turtle', but I had no idea what kind of turtle. I'm not even sure I knew there were different kinds of turtles. Many years later I came to understand that we had

had an up close and personal interaction with an 'ornate box turtle' (*Terrapene ornata*). Currently, this turtle species is listed as 'Threatened and Species of Greatest Conservation Need' in Iowa. Since that time, I have, literally, walked many hundreds of miles in Iowa woodlands. I have never seen another ornate box turtle in the wild. Who knew that I had reached the zenith of my ornate box turtle experience as an eight-year-old? You just never know what you might find wandering around out in nature – or whether you'll ever see it again.

# Bugs and Snakes

*Two roads diverged in a yellow wood*

Robert Frost

Like many young humans, I was fascinated by the world around me, especially the many creatures that were not humans. Watching huge flocks of small birds flying around as the fall migration began. Reading about the incredibly large blue whales (*Balaenoptera musculus*) in my family's set of 'children's encyclopedias'. Noticing that the two apple trees (*Malus domestica*) in our backyard, while both being 'apple trees' produced fruits that looked, and tasted, quite different. I was amazed by the diversity that I was surrounded by, though I certainly didn't know the word 'biodiversity'. I might not even have known the word 'biology' as science was seen as a rather low priority in the Catholic school I attended.

One summer, I started noticing 'bugs', mostly insects (Class Insecta), with a few spiders (Class Arachnida) and isopods (Class Malacostraca) thrown in for good measure. I fashioned a 'bug net' from a forked stick and pillowcase I 'borrowed' from the linen drawer. I spent much of the summer catching butterflies (Order Lepidoptera), which when you think about it, really should be called 'flutter bys', beetles (Order Coleoptera), and bees and wasps (Order Hymenoptera), which was a more 'high stakes' endeavor. I wasn't, yet, familiar with 'collections-based' research, so as I recall, all of these creatures were returned to the wild after inspection. Using a book about insects that I repeatedly checked out from the Bookmobile, which parked once a week on the street corner west of our house, I was able to identify a few of the bugs I captured. My most impressive, and memorable, catches were an eastern tiger swallowtail butterfly (*Papilio glaucus*) and huge cecropia moth (*Hyalophora cecropia*). But most of the creatures I caught could be identified, with the experience and resources available, only as a 'beetle', or a 'moth', or a 'spider'. Later in life, my daughter and I spent an entire summer making an 'insect collection'. We were able to put names on many more of the creatures we captured, and we kept them in boxes to amaze grandparents and friends. My daughter did not grow up to be a biologist, but she doesn't say 'eeeww' every time she sees an insect either. Experience and knowledge of the natural world can often lead to interest and respect.

With all due respect to bugs, my true passion became reptiles and amphibians. Interacting with amphibians was easy. There was a pond nearby that my friends and I would walk to with the express intention of catching frogs. We didn't do anything with the frogs, we just released them back to the pond. The point was to learn to catch them and be able to look closely at them as they blinked their large eyes. The frogs in question were mostly northern leopard frogs (*Lithobates pipiens*). My reflexes may be insufficient today, but I still remember the approach. Spot a frog's head poking up out of the water. Get down on hands and knees along the very edge of the pond and approach the frog slowly. Slowly point one arm straight out, low, above the pond water, and then, very slowly bend your elbow to bring that hand up behind the frog. Just before you thought the frog was going to dip beneath the surface of the water and be gone forever, grab the frog as quickly as possible. The approach was not always successful but worked often enough to keep us entertained for hours. I'm guessing the frogs felt rather differently.

Interacting with reptiles was a different matter. Iowa does not have a great diversity of reptiles, and they are generally well concealed and considerably 'feistier' than frogs. One of our most common turtles was the snapping turtle (*Chelydra serpentina*), a species that, in general, we actively tried to avoid, although we did find some hatchlings emerging from their nest on a sandbar one time that we examined closely. We focused on snakes. Most of Iowa's snakes are non-venomous and the venomous species are very rare. I have never seen a venomous snake in Iowa. Snakes are hard to find, so we'd walk around a lot in the summer woodlands and grassy areas of our part of Iowa seeking them out. By 'them' I mean the one species of snake we could actually find: the common garter snake (*Thamnophis sirtalis*). We would occasionally catch one and began to develop a sense of what constituted good garter snake habitat. Sometimes, we'd bring one home and keep it in captivity for a while to share its awesomeness with family and friends. We'd also put sacrificial field crickets (members of the Family Gryllidae) into the cage to observe feeding behavior of the snake. My father made me a 'snake cage' with a latch on top. If one forgets to fasten the latch, and the snake ends up in a laundry basket, one's mother forbids any further captive snakes in the basement.

Sadly, I did not grow up to be a 'herpetologist'. The road not taken. But my fascination with snakes continued. I have had the opportunity to hold a few species of snakes, including western fox snakes (*Pantherophis ramspotti*), northern water snakes (*Nerodia sipedon*), ring-necked snakes (*Diadophis punctatus*), western ribbon snakes (*Thamnophis proximus*), and tiny brown snakes (*Storeria dekayi*). I also was fortunate enough to observe a large prairie rattlesnake (*Crotalus viridis*) crawl slowly across a trail in the low elevation foothills of Colorado. Once my three-year-old son was safely perched on my shoulders, I was much more comfortable. But I had no desire to hold the rattlesnake. Still, there is something very engaging about being in close proximity to animals that could seriously injure or kill you.

Not being a herpetologist did nothing to diminish my desire to share my fascination with snakes. I led numerous early fall field trips, with biology students, to a nearby location that had woodlands, flooded oxbows, reconstructed prairie, and wetlands. Great Iowa snake habitat. The oxbows, in particular, were home to numerous, and large, northern water snakes. On one such adventure, we had managed to find, and catch, a few snakes, including garter snakes, brown snakes, and fox snakes. For many of the students this presented them with an opportunity to hold a snake for the first time in their lives. There was initial hesitance from some, but I don't remember anyone ever saying that they were sorry that they had held a snake. Looking into the eyes of a snake it's easy to imagine them sizing you up as to whether or not they could swallow you whole. They are very serious and dedicated predators.

As the afternoon was winding down, and we were beginning to head back to our vehicles by walking along the edge of an oxbow, I spotted a rather unusual sight. A good-sized northern water snake was sunning itself on a grassy hummock fully out of the water. I motioned to the students to be quiet and stay where they were. I stealthily approached the snake, and then, imagining that I was much younger than I actually was, I dove and grabbed the snake. Unfortunately, I grabbed it quite a bit further behind its head than I intended. As I struggled to stand back up, it bit me several times before I could get a better grip. An interesting fact about northern water snakes is that their saliva contains an anticoagulant which causes their bites to bleed rather impressively. My left arm was dripping blood. But they are beautiful snakes, and well worth a bite or two to observe closely. The light-colored underside of the snake typically has striking reddish crescents of color. I offered, repeatedly, to let students hold the snake. Sadly, none took me up on the offer, probably passing up a 'once in a lifetime' opportunity.

# Fishing

*Fishing is not just about catching fish; it's about understanding the delicate balance of nature.*

Aldo Leopold

My mom really liked camping, my dad less so. We didn't have much money, and my dad had little vacation time that was not taken up by home improvement projects. So, they bought a small pop-up tent trailer camper and for one week each summer we would take a family camping vacation. Two parents, five children, and one beagle. We did not go to 'exotic locales'. Nearby state forests or parks were our typical destinations. I was still very excited about the prospect each summer because of two introduced species that were present at our intended destinations: rainbow trout (*Oncorhynchus mykiss*) and brown trout (*Salmo trutta*).

The river I fished at home had sluggish muddy brown water (although sometimes the water was reddish immediately downstream of the local meat packing plant). The river was home to channel catfish (*Ictalurus punctatus*) and common carp (*Cyprinus carpio*), amongst other fish species that we rarely saw, though I once caught a short-nosed gar (*Lepisosteus platostomus*). There were also smooth softshell turtles (*Apalone mutica*), and in places, numerous freshwater mussels that we could find by wading barefoot in the murky river. During the summer I would ride my bicycle, while wearing a backpack with fishing gear and holding a fishing rod gripped tightly against the right handlebar of my bike, a few miles down to the river. The last mile was all downhill, which was always less fun on the way home in the late afternoon heat. There was a low head dam on that stretch of the river that tended to concentrate fish, and my friends and I spent many sultry summer afternoons near there messing with tangled up, or broken, fishing gear and, occasionally, catching fish. We often targeted common carp as they were really fun to catch on our lightweight and generally substandard fishing poles. We made a 'special' type of dough ball bait, the recipe of which has been lost to time, but as I recall included stale bread, peanut butter, cinnamon, and bacon grease, to attract carp. In and around slapping mosquitoes and losing fish because we weren't very good at tying the knots used to attach our hooks to the fishing line, we had a great time.

Late in the summer the designated week for the family vacation would arrive. After what seemed like hours of packing and grumbling, our station wagon was loaded with family, dog, and supplies, and pulling the trailer behind, we would finally roll out of our driveway and head northeast. My mind was filled with visions of glistening trout leaping out of water so clear that you could actually see the bottom. I had prepared carefully. Newspaper route money had been used to put a new line on my Zebco 202 fishing reel. I had also purchased two new lures: small, pounded metal spoons, one brass colored and one silver colored. I was equal parts excited and confident.

The drive always seemed very long, but it was only a couple hours. Wind blasting through open windows to cool us down under the hot sun blazing in the summer sky. Small town after small town. Field after field of corn or soybeans. The occasional herd of cattle or group of hogs wandering around in green pastures. Dead, flattened, snakes in the road. Finally, we started to pass through much hillier country with winding ridge tops dropping down into deep valleys past occasional limestone outcrops. And then, at last, the sign announcing we'd entered the state forest. Thrilling. A few more curves of the winding road and we entered the campground. A constantly changing small, densely populated, city of camper trailers, tents, and vehicles. People coming and going on various missions. We had favorite campsites of course which, typically, were already occupied by someone else. My parents' main goal was to find a spot that was unoccupied and had one or more tall trees for shade. My main goal was to find a spot as near as possible to the trout stream that meandered through the state forest camping area. My goal was, at best, a very distant third priority. We found a spot with shade a long way from the stream.

I probably tried to help set up camp. I'm sure I must have. But I had an intense desire to catch trout. These were fish that didn't even exist in the river I usually fished. This one week was my only chance to catch trout over the entire course of a year. I had spotted a bend in the creek that I thought looked great for trout while we'd been driving around seeking a spot to set up camp. Likely, I asked politely and respectfully, perhaps more than once, whether I had done enough chores and if someone could drive me back to that spot so that I could fulfill the single most important aspect of the family vacation – start catching trout. Finally, no doubt persuaded by the compelling logic of my argument, my dad told me to get my 'damn pole' and he'd take me.

I sat on the edge of the front seat, directing my dad back to the location that I suspected had numerous, and no doubt large, trout, probably of both species. My dad found a wide spot along the edge of the gravel road, and I hopped out and grabbed my fishing pole from the back seat. It was shady under the trees by the road, but the air was thick, warm, and humid. Wearing shorts felt very good. There was only a narrow band of vegetation separating me from the stream and all of those trout. With the exuberance of youth, I charged forward, fishing pole in hand.

At first there was just a slight burning sensation on my exposed thighs and shins. By the time I had reached the stream this had blossomed to full-fledged burning and itching. Visual inspection revealed the presence of numerous white bumps on the skin of my legs. The pain intensified in a rather shocking way, and I knelt down in the cold spring fed stream to try to minimize the burning and itching. It worked somewhat, but mostly it just took some time. Perhaps twenty minutes or so, though it seemed much longer. This proved to be an effective, and memorable, introduction to the plant species known as 'wood nettle' (*Laportea canadensis*). It is a truly remarkable plant that produces 'stinging hairs'. These hairs have a sharp, fragile, tip with a mixture of skin irritant chemicals that are produced in a gland, and importantly, are under pressure. So, the series of events is: 1) sharp tip penetrates skin; 2) body part moves, thereby breaking off the fragile tip; 3) contents, under pressure, are squirted into the skin – acting much like a hypodermic needle; and 4) burning, itching, and blistering ensues. Ignorance can be bliss, but ignorance can also be blisters. Being able to identify wood nettle (and its equally annoying relative 'stinging nettle', *Urtica dioica*) would have allowed me to detour around them. Wearing long pants, and walking slowly though the nettles, would have allowed me to avoid their nasty little stinging hairs. It turns out that 'knowing the neighbors' (especially the annoying ones) can be quite useful.

After the burning and stinging subsided somewhat I stood up and made a mental note of what the plants I had just walked through looked like. About thigh high. Dark green. Oval leaves with toothed margins. Lots of small, shiny, pointed hairs. Unpleasant experience can be a good teacher. A few casts later, my pounded metal silver spoon flashing in the current of clear water, I hooked a fish. I lifted it out of the water. It was not a rainbow trout. It was not a brown trout. At the time I had no idea what it was. I now know it was a creek chub (*Semotilus atromaculatus*). A perfectly respectable, and unlike the trout, native fish species found in Iowa's streams. I was confused and disappointed. I released the chub, flailed the water with numerous casts, but caught no trout. Eventually, I treated the wood nettle with newfound respect and joined my dad in the car for the ride back to camp.

The next day one of our favorite campsites opened up. It was the last campsite at the end of the access road and was favored by the presence of a very large tree that, had I known more about the neighbors at the time, I would have recognized as a 'cottonwood' (*Populus deltoides*) tree. Even better, MUCH better, the campsite was right next to the stream. We rapidly broke camp and moved there. Reasoning that my silver spoon had caught some kind of fish that I knew wasn't a trout, I cut the line and painstakingly tied on the bronze spoon and walked down to the creek, taking care to notice the prevailing vegetation even though I was wearing long pants. The clear water was gurgling rapidly through a rocky riffle angling toward the bank opposite where I was standing. At the downstream end of the riffle there was a cut bank overhanging a small pool of darker, deeper, water. After a couple of miss-aimed casts I landed the spoon right in the pool. In an instant a fish flashed out from under the overhanging bank and hit the spoon. I felt the surge of the fish pulling on the line. And then, almost as quickly, the line went slack. I was crushed – I was sure it had been a trout and from the brief glimpse I had gotten a very nice one. I casted numerous times. Upstream of the pool and let the spoon tumble in. Downstream of the pool dragging the spoon through the pool against the current. Nothing. I knew that if I casted too close to the cut bank and snagged the spoon on one of the many exposed roots and then had to wade in to get it I would never catch that trout. But I casted again as close to the bank as I dared.

The spoon fluttered as it fell through the water. The trout ate the spoon and the two of us were firmly connected by a thin line of monofilament. The fish jumped out of the water and fought with all its might for its life, but I brought it in and slid it up on the bank. It was beautiful. A shining rainbow trout. I picked it up and ran back to our campsite to show everyone. My mom helped me clean it and wrapped it in aluminum foil before placing it on coals from our campfire. It was delicious and my connection to the neighbors grew stronger with each bite.

# Mountain Men

*I didn't think it proper to spoilt* [sic] *a good story just for the sake of the truth.*

Jim Bridger

As was typical for a summer afternoon between my freshman and sophomore years of high school, my friend and I walked to the grocery store and bought some candy before heading back up the hill to the grounds surrounding our old elementary school. There was a large sugar maple (*Acer saccharum*) on the property with low spreading branches that was easy to climb up into and sit comfortably, well hidden from prying eyes by the dark green maple leaves. By the end of our undistinguished elementary school careers, we had both devoured all the books in the school library covering the topic of 'mountain men of the old west'. Names such as 'Jim Bridger', 'Tom Fitzpatrick' and 'Jedidiah Smith' were commonly heard in our conversations. I'm pretty sure that both of us thought being a mountain man was still a viable career option.

Our tree branch conversation turned to how we might start pursuing our chosen career, and, in a stroke of genius, we hit upon the idea that we could start NOW by trapping for fur right here in Iowa. Clearly, that would be excellent preparation for our future as mountain men. As luck would have it, the father of one of our other friends had been a fur trapper when he was younger. He was a 'crusty old coot', but we recruited our other friend into our grand plan and were soon talking with his dad about trapping. We had already spent years hiking around exploring our local rivers and streams and had a pretty good idea of where we could set out trap lines. We pooled our paper route, odd job, and 'allowance' money and started buying traps. Number 1 Victor long spring leg hold traps for muskrats (*Ondatra zibethicus*). Number 2 Victor coil spring leg hold traps for raccoons (*Procyon lotor*). A few 110 Conibear kill traps for muskrats and mink (*Neogale vison*). We practiced setting the traps in my childhood sandbox while trying to avoid getting our fingers pinched.

As summer neared an end, the pace of our preparations increased. Many days would soon be spent non-productively at school. We had read that new traps needed to be boiled in water with walnut (*Juglans regia*) husks to remove the unnatural smells of metal and oil. A neighbor let us pick up walnuts in their yard and my mom loaned us a large metal wash tub in which to carry out the task. We learned about using 'fish oil' as an attractant for raccoons. Production of fish oil required catching some carp (*Cyprinus carpio*), chopping them into chunks, placing them in a large glass jar, adding a bit of water, putting the lid on tightly and burying the jar in the ground for a month. I'm not sure we actually produced fish oil, but we did produce something with an exceptionally powerful smell. We went to the local hardware store where we always bought our fishing licenses and proudly announced that we would be needing trapping licenses. We read through the trapping regulations and carefully noted the day that trapping season began – the first Saturday in November. It dawned on us that, in November, the water in the river would be pretty chilly. We spent more of our limited budget on the cheapest hip waders we could find.

With the trapping season only a couple of weeks away, we talked our friend's dad into taking a hike with us to 'show us a few things', although as teenagers we were pretty much sure we knew everything already. We walked along the edge of the river and the streams we were planning to trap and learned how to tell mink tracks from raccoon tracks and what muskrat tracks and muskrat scat looked like. We saw 'beaver (*Castor canadensis*) slides' where they were dragging willow (*Salix* species) trees they had cut down on the bank back into the water. I also learned about 'beggarticks' (members of the genus *Bidens*), native plants that produce fruits (each containing one seed) with two barbed bristles that stick very tightly in cotton socks exposed by wearing jeans one has significantly outgrown. After blissful ignorance allowed me to walk through a dense patch of beggarticks, my ankles looked like twin porcupines. My friend's dad pointed out some spots that might be good to place a trap. We learned that placing a trap takes considerable thought and knowledge about the animal you're trying to trap. You're trying to predict exactly where an inherently unpredictable animal will place one of its four feet, or for a kill trap, its head. Baits and scent lures can help a lot, but they are no substitute for knowing a lot about what behaviors a particular species of animal is likely to exhibit.

None of us were old enough to drive, so on opening day we put on our hip waders, hefted our battered old packs that were full of traps, wire, trap stakes, wire cutters, a hatchet, carefully sealed up fish oil, a few sundries, and mounted our trusty bicycles. Mine was a black one-speed coaster brake bike with a 'banana seat' and high-rise handlebars. Likely, we looked even 'cooler' than the description sounds. We spent much of the day making sets in places where muskrats were depositing scat and under overhanging stream banks that we thought mink might pass through looking for a meal. We made 'cubby' sets for raccoons baited with fish oil. We returned home late in the afternoon, tired but confident.

Four AM on Sunday arrived much earlier than a teenaged boy might expect. It was also quite a bit darker than one might have thought. We assembled from our various homes and pedaled off in the dark, with no lights of any kind on our bikes. It was brisk coasting down the long hill to the river. Because we knew that time would be limited on days when we had to attend school, we had divided the trapline into three parts, one portion for each of us. First one of my friends departed to check traps along a small tributary of the river. Then my other friend said goodbye and went to check traps on his portion of the river. Finally, I hid my bike in a road ditch, turned on my handheld flashlight and stumbled down the steep bank to the river.

Other than the murmuring of the water flowing in the river, it was quiet. Until it wasn't. A barred owl (*Strix varia*) sounded off with a very loud 'Who Cooks for You' in the tree right above me. After the uncontrollable trembling stopped, I opened my eyes. It was still very dark. Somehow it seemed even darker with my flashlight on and my vision restricted to its narrow, rather weak, beam of light. Exactly where we had set the first trap had seemed very clear yesterday, but much less so now. After a few cases of mistaken identity, I located the first trap. It was still sitting just as we'd left it. On to the next trap, and the next, and the next. Clearly, something was wrong. I hadn't caught anything. Finally, it was back up the riverbank to the gravel road to walk back to my bike. My pack was empty. Not a single trap had even been snapped in a failed attempt to catch something. I pedaled back down the road in the growing light of dawn and saw my friend waiting for me. Nothing. We pedaled together back to our other friend who had also caught nothing. This puzzled us. In our previous readings, Jim Bridger had always caught at least one beaver. We were trying, and failing, to catch species much more numerous than beavers. We headed back up the hill to home and breakfast.

And so went our first week as trappers. Up at four AM. Ride our bikes to the river. Not catch anything. Ride back home. Eat breakfast, clean up (maybe), and catch the bus to school. The four AM thing was definitely cutting into our nightlife of doing homework. The next weekend my friend's dad agreed to take a look at our sets and see if he could provide any help. Under his gentle guidance ('you guys are idiots') we made some modifications to our approach. Eventually, we started to catch a few. A muskrat or two, here, a raccoon there, none of the less numerous and considerably more wary mink. Maybe it was the gentle guidance, but more likely it was one of the most important lessons to be learned in trapping and, for that matter, in life generally. Patience matters. Eventually, an unlucky muskrat, who had probably been walking near one of our traps for days, stepped in the wrong place. All of this success, of course, led to another problem. What do you do when you actually catch something? So, we had to learn to skin, flesh, stretch, and dry our furs. None of us had any previous experience beyond cleaning a fish. My friend's dad, who was 'crusty', was also generous. He allowed us to use his garage as our 'fur shed' and agreed to show us how to skin an animal to remove its pelt. He taught us how to get our knives sharp and where to start the skinning process. He provided helpful tips along the way ('not like that you dumb**s'), and eventually we got good at 'skinning out' muskrats and raccoons. We made fur stretchers from the slats of old peach crates and hung the fur up in his garage to dry (and smell funky).

As the season progressed and our confidence began to slowly return, we felt that we were ready for new challenges. The weather was turning colder with the shortening of the days, and having water flow down the back of your legs after over-topping your hip waders was getting less funny. We were pleased to learn that Iowa had recently opened a beaver season that had been closed for many years. The season had been closed for many years because overharvest and habitat destruction had dramatically decreased the population of beavers in the state. Beavers were probably never 'extirpated' (made locally extinct) in Iowa, but there hadn't been many of them. Now the population had recovered somewhat, and the trapping season was to start the following weekend. This got our attention, of course, because any career as a mountain man would definitely require being well versed in trapping beavers. We had no traps suitable for beavers, so we made another capital investment and bought two Number 4 Victor double long spring leg hold traps and one Conibear 330 kill trap. The leg hold traps were just larger versions of what we were routinely using. We'd gotten familiar enough with such traps that we could easily set them even with ice water numbed fingers. The 330 Conibear was just plain frightening. Any trap that could kill a beaver could also easily break a teenage boy's arm. My friend's dad taught us how to set it and helpfully added 'don't get your arm caught in it'.

On the morning beaver season opened, it was chilly, dark, and pouring rain. Your father's old cotton parka smells funny when it's soaking wet. All three of us were working on setting out the beaver traps. We had found a place with recent beaver activity on one of the streams we trapped. There were recently cut down trees, what we suspected was a bank den entrance, and a larger log, partially chewed through by a beaver on the edge of a sandbar that sloped gently into deeper water toward the other side of the creek. We thought we'd get the 330 set first and place it in the suspected den entrance. The three of us were in a triangle around the trap. Flashlight beams were at various angles with rain drops zipping through the light beams. We got the springs compressed and were attempting to release the safeties, when... Well, I'm not really sure what happened. The trap tipped over and fell on the ground, the trigger was released, and the trap jumped up in the air between the three of us up to about waist height. We immediately decided we'd set up the 330 on a day when it wasn't raining. Or maybe never. That left the two leg hold traps. We set one at the bottom of a beaver slide and one right where the beaver had been chewing through that larger log. The leg hold traps were wired to metal fence poles that we had pounded into the bottom of the creek, using the hammer side of our hatchets, in water as deep as we dared to go with our hip waders. Then it was time to walk back to the bikes and make our soggy ride back up the hill to thaw out at home.

The next morning was a Sunday, cool but not raining. One of my friends wasn't able to go that day, but two of us set off on our bikes. We had other traps to check before we got to the beaver sets, but we didn't catch anything. At the farthest point upstream from where our bikes were hidden, we got to the beaver sets. We could see the trap at the bottom of the beaver slide was undisturbed. The trap by the log, however, was gone. We both knew two things: 1) beavers can hold their breath for a long time under water; and 2) beavers have really big teeth. It was still fully dark, not even a hint of pre-dawn light yet. We proceeded slowly, and carefully, into the water holding nothing more lethal than a stout stick. We shuffled our feet carefully on the sandy bottom, ready to rapidly retreat at the first sign of attack. Eventually, I tried to set my foot down on the bottom – and it didn't make it all the way down. I'm guessing there was some adrenaline involved, but eventually I reached down into the ice-cold water and found the trap wire, with a dead beaver attached. We were actual beaver trappers!

As is often the case in life, success begets new problems. The beaver was a full-grown adult. It would not fit in either of our packs. We needed to cross the creek, walk through some woods to get to the road, and then walk to our bikes. With each of us holding the beaver by one rear leg we were able, with some effort, to reach our bikes. The stream we were on was over a mile, mostly uphill, from my house. The beaver would not fit in our packs. We couldn't ride our bikes with each of us holding on to one rear leg. Inspiration struck – we could wire the beaver's legs over the bike's crossbar and ride home that way. As it turns out, balance is a very important part of riding a bicycle. A beaver (weighing, we learned later, 44 pounds) swaying back and forth on the crossbar unrecoverably upsets any attempt at balance. We walked and pushed our bikes up the hill to home with a large beaver dangling from the crossbar of my bike. I was very late getting to my Sunday morning paper route. But – I didn't care, I was one beaver closer to Jim Bridger's lifetime total. That was as close as I ever got.

# Ice and Fire

*Life is not a matter of holding good cards but sometimes playing a poor hand well.*

Jack London

Once the cold of winter really set in, our favorite creek became a highway that we could explore for miles. It was a great way to spend a Saturday when the shackles of school were temporarily removed. We learned that ice right along the shore was often thin, and we learned that areas with fast current often had thin (or no) ice. We learned to walk with a shuffling gait on bare ice to minimize the chance of slipping and falling. It was interesting to see the tracks of various animals in the snow on the ice or the shoreline. The first time I ever saw a white-tailed deer (*Odocoileus virginianus*) track was on one of these winter hikes. It may seem odd that, having reached the age of 16 or so, I was just now seeing a deer track. The explanation is that unregulated hunting had nearly extirpated deer from Iowa by the early 1900s. The deer population was slowly beginning to increase. It would continue to do so until Iowa became the envy of white-tailed deer hunters across the country.

One sunny and cold winter day I went for a hike with my younger brother and our two cousins, who were between my brother and I in age. I figured that part of the job of being a 'mountain man' would be to serve as a guide for those who were less knowledgeable.

So, I routinely practiced on my siblings and relatives. Our goal for that day was to explore a region of the creek that we had not been in before. We left our house and walked past schools and residential areas, finally passing some businesses and industrial sites before emerging into the edge of the county fairgrounds. We accessed the creek by walking through a thin strip of woods. I picked up a stout stick that had been stripped of its bark by a beaver (*Castor canadensis*) and I told my brother and cousins to wait on the bank while I 'checked out' the ice. Fancying myself to be quite an 'ice-spert', I took a couple of steps onto the ice, hit the ice a couple of times with the butt end of the stick and pronounced it to be 'good ice'. The others joined me, and we started walking upstream. It was always interesting to see new parts of the creek, to not know what was around the next bend. After walking for a while, we noticed that the far side of the creek had what appeared to be a significantly larger woodland. Definitely worthy of investigation.

We started to cross the creek, with me going first, my brother next, and my cousins following. We were heading toward an 'outside bend' where the water depth would be the greatest, though on this stream that was still unlikely to be more than waist deep. As I got close to the far bank the ice made some concerning sounds, but I made it ashore. My brother was close behind. One cousin joined us and then the other cousin yelped in terror as the ice broke and he dropped through into the water below. He yelled 'I can't touch the bottom' as he tried to get a grip on the slippery ice. I stepped back onto the ice until I was close enough to grab his hand and pull him out onto the ice. He hadn't been in the water long, but it was plenty long enough for his blue jeans, cotton socks, and boots to be completely soaked. He was scared, we were miles from home, and it was cold. Probably not 'below zero' Fahrenheit, but not far from it. It turned out that, although I was somewhat knowledgeable about ice, there were a couple of things that I was unaware of. First, ice becomes 'fatigued' with repeated stress. If the ice is thick that doesn't matter much to a person on foot, but if the ice is thin, it can certainly matter to the last person in line. Second, just upstream, around the next bend, there was an outfall of wastewater from an industrial plant that emptied into the creek. This water was much warmer than the water in the creek, which of course, leads to thin ice. We never walked on the ice in that part of the creek again.

We climbed the bank into the woods, no longer with the intention of exploring, but simply of finding a good spot to build a fire. My cousin stood shivering as the rest of us gathered firewood without the benefit of having a saw. Always bring a saw, you never know when you might need it. I cleared away the snow in a spot next to a fallen log where my cousin could sit and proceeded to start the fire. I was actually quite skilled at building fires, in part because I always carried what we called 'paper birch bark' in my fire kit. The bark made excellent tinder, but it was actually thin, tattered, pieces of bark from 'river birch' trees (*Betula nigra*), not from 'paper birch' trees (*Betula papyrifera*), which were not present in our woodlands. A case of 'mistaken identity'. We quickly had a warm blaze going. I had my cousin take off his boots, socks, and jeans. I took off my parka and wool shirt to help keep him warm while we burned holes in his jeans, socks, and boots trying to dry them out. After a while, he warmed up and we all started enjoying the day again as we continued to throw wood on the fire. We decided it was probably best if we didn't tell his mother what had happened.

After a couple of hours my cousin put on his thoroughly smoked jeans, socks, and boots. They had several new holes and were still damp, but they were no longer soaking wet. We decided not to recross the creek on the ice, but rather to head upstream to a set of railroad tracks that had a bridge over the creek. Along the way we discovered the warm water outflow and put two and two together. After climbing up the railroad embankment, my cousins and I crossed the railroad bridge, carefully stepping on the ties and trying to ignore the openings between the ties that allowed a clear view to the creek that was surprisingly far below us. After crossing, we looked back and my brother was still on the other side of the bridge. He was eight or nine at that point, clearly old enough to be out walking on ice and on railroad tracks with no supervision beyond his older brother. Cajoling had no effect on starting him across the bridge. I had to go back across to him. There were tears in his eyes and he was scared. I carried him across to the far side of the bridge, probably with the admonition of 'don't tell Mom about this'. My brother grew up to do far scarier things, things that would terrify me, such as rolling his kayak upside down and popping upright again on the other side, but on that day, he needed a helping hand.

One might think that such an experience would have ended my traveling on ice career. It didn't. And, with few exceptions, I mostly stayed on the dry side of the ice. Most of the exceptions were minor. One leg popping through the ice up to my knee. Unpleasant, but not life-threatening, sometimes eliciting a wry chuckle. There was also the occasional less funny 'both legs up to the thigh' type immersion. But one event stands out clearly in my mind. I was on a January winter camping trip in Quetico Park in southwest Ontario. My friend and I were skiing down a winding river doing a 'recon' to try to figure out in what direction we should move our camp next. The snow was just a couple inches deep on the ice, and it was warm, in the 20s above zero Fahrenheit. I was going first downstream, and then, I wasn't going at all. I had dropped right through a weak spot in the ice, skis and all. I was in water to my upper chest and could not touch the bottom. Somehow the buoyancy afforded by wind-proof shell garments, the strength of youth, and the immediate shot of adrenaline, resulted in me pushing down on the edge of the ice in front of me and rolling out of the hole with my skis attached. I slid away from the hole, stood up, and shook myself off. My friend skied up to me and said "wow, you got out really quickly… I didn't even have time to take a picture." I said, "I'm not getting back in – take a picture of the hole." We completed our recon before heading back to camp where I changed into my spare set of clothes. After that day, the bottom dropped out and it got quite cold, at least thirty degrees below zero every morning. My ski boots, which were completely soaked, froze solid every time I took them off. The next morning, I had to tie the laces together and wear them around my neck under my parka to thaw them out enough to get them on my feet. Anyway, frozen lakes and streams present great avenues for travel. I enthusiastically recommend them. Just be ready for when you fall through.

# Upland Birds

*Guns and dogs don't kill grouse, legs do.*

Frank Woolner

I made a new friend during my first semester of graduate school in Wisconsin. He was more or less my 'boss' too, but that didn't seem to matter much. In casual conversation I had learned that he was a hunter. I told him that I was a hunter too. Strictly speaking that was true. I had been hunting. I'd brought home a few fox squirrels (*Sciurus niger*), a couple of cottontail rabbits (*Sylvilagus floridanus*), and, rather amazingly, one bobwhite quail (*Colinus virginianus*) that I had shot with my very own gun – a single shot, break action, Ithaca .410 shotgun. But to be honest, I had not grown up in a hunting family and in actuality I had very little hunting experience. I had walked along on a couple of ring-necked pheasant (*Phasianus colchicus*) hunts without ever firing a shot. I had never been white-tailed deer (*Odocoileus virginianus*) hunting, or knew anybody who did go deer hunting. The majority of my experience was in the similar, but quite distinct, skill set of trapping, which I had given up several years prior. Still, I was very happy to say 'yes' when my new friend invited me to go ruffed grouse (*Bonasa umbellus*) hunting with him. Little did I know what a major impact this bird species would have on my life, and on the lives of some of those I was to interact with in the future.

I made the trek back to Iowa to borrow my dad's 12-gauge bolt action J.C. Higgins shotgun. It's not a 'collector's item'. He didn't mind parting with it, and I still have it, though I never use it. As the grouse season was nearing its end my friend and I identified a weekend day that the weather was acceptable and that we both had time. It was a cold, sunny day with a few inches of snow on the ground. On the drive to our destination, I questioned my friend extensively as to what ruffed grouse looked like because I had never seen one, whether it was legal to shoot both males and females, and how one could recognize grouse tracks. My friend had two German Shorthair Pointers. One of these dogs would hunt ONLY with my friend, the other dog wouldn't really hunt with anybody, though you were welcome to try to keep up. That's the dog I hunted with.

We were hunting in the 'coulee region' of southwest Wisconsin. Ridges steep enough, but not tall enough, to be mountains interspersed with deep valleys hosting rocky bottomed streams. Unlike the pheasants I had known in Iowa, which are grassland birds, ruffed grouse are birds of the forest, especially young, thick forests. The dogs wore collars with bells on them. The idea was to follow the sound of the bell. When the bell stopped ringing the idea was to find the (now silent) dog because it might be pointing a grouse. Or not. So, walk up the ridge, then down the ridge, then back up the ridge. Listen for the bell. Plow through blackberry (members of the genus *Rubus*) brambles. Wonder which direction the dog is in before faintly hearing a bell in the opposite direction you expected. Find a thicket of 'prickly ash' (*Zanthoxylum americanum*), a thorny understory shrub that, heretofore, I had been blissfully unaware of, and passing through it I tore both skin and fabric. Just another neighbor it would be best to avoid. And then, repeat throughout the day. I loved it. I'm not sure I even saw a grouse that day, but my friend, who had grown up grouse hunting, got two and while we were cleaning the birds in the fading daylight, he gave me one to take home. It was delicious.

I never shot a grouse that season, but by the time the next fall had rolled around, my friend and I had become good buddies, and I was planning to do a lot more grouse hunting. I did not have the ideal grouse shotgun. A previously invisible grouse blasting off the ground with thundering wings and flying quickly through trees rarely gives one the chance to work a bolt action to get a second shot. At least I had a first shot. The grouse population was good that year. We were seeing grouse regularly, though rarely more than just a quick glimpse of brown wings flapping frantically through the trees. I shot a lot of saplings. It quickly became apparent that not only was I not an 'instinctive' wing shot, but I had also never actually practiced wing shooting. Still, most grouse hunting was just walking around in the woods, and I was good at that. My friend continued to get grouse fairly regularly, and I just kept going.

It was a cloudy day in late November, and I had been working my way up a ridge that I thought the dog had gone up, though I could no longer hear the bell. I saw some conifers higher up on the ridge and walked toward them. As I got closer, I heard wings and got a brief glimpse of a grouse flying out of one of the conifers. There was no shot opportunity, but I had seen the direction the bird was flying, and I headed that way. There was also a one-in-threehundred-and-sixty-degree chance the dog was in that direction. I noticed a deadfall of tangled branches up ahead of me through the woods and headed for it. Just as I came up to the deadfall, a grouse flushed on the opposite side and flew straight away from me with no trees in between us. I raised my shotgun, squeezed the trigger, never felt the recoil at all, and the grouse dropped, wings flopping, to the forest floor. It was unclear who was more surprised, me or the grouse. What was clear was that I was now completely 'hooked' on upland bird hunting. I picked up the grouse. Its weight felt great in my hand as I admired its sharply pointed beak, black eyes, and the range of tan, brown, white, and black feathers covering its now limp body. I headed down the ridge to find my friend and show him that

I had finally succeeded. Over the next couple years, I hunted with my friend until he moved away and, sadly, took his dogs with him. I had managed to work my way up to being a 'mediocre' grouse hunter and occasionally brought home woodcock (*Scolopax minor*) as well. I felt like, and identified as, an 'upland bird hunter', but it would be a while before I became active again in that pursuit.

After moving back to Iowa years later, I fully intended to rapidly re-activate my upland bird hunting career. Life, however, was busy with children, a demanding job, and family responsibilities. But eventually I got a dog – a female yellow Labrador retriever – and quickly realized I had little idea of where to go pheasant hunting in the local area, and not much understanding of how to be successful at pheasant hunting. During my first Iowa pheasant season I only went hunting a few times and managed to bring home a grand total of one rooster (a male pheasant) home for dinner. My dog found the rooster I had shot a few rows into a standing corn field, but she didn't bite it or retrieve it. I simply found her, and therefore, the pheasant. I figured that was a one-time thing. As it turned out, that dog would retrieve anything except birds and to my knowledge she never grabbed a bird with her mouth. In later years she would lay down on pheasants and wait for me to find her. I took to calling her a 'Labrador Retreater', but she never showed any sign of being ashamed.

The years passed bringing more dogs (all labs – all of which did retrieve birds), more days spent 'wading' for miles through thick pheasant cover, more understanding of good local places to go hunting and the habitats in which pheasants were most likely to be. This resulted in more pheasants being brought home for dinner. I tried to get my kids interested in hunting pheasants. They weren't interested. I tried out a few potential hunting buddies but didn't find a good fit of available time or interest. Mostly, I hunted on my own and learned in the 'school of hard knocks'. Slowly it happened.

I had become a 'good', way above average, pheasant hunter. I had morphed into 'hunting mentor' material. Friends who were good hunters, but not upland bird hunters, learned from me about the importance of 'not hurrying' your shot when a rooster flushes and surprises you. You have more time (a little) than you think. Students, and ex-students, learned from me how to recognize good pheasant habitat, and how that might change depending on the weather and time of year. Cattail marshes can be great for pheasants when it's cold and snowy but are much less likely to hold pheasants on a warm early season day. They also learned how to clean pheasants and that pheasant legs make great soup stock. Children of friends learned from me about aspects of public land hunting etiquette. If there's already a vehicle in the parking lot, go somewhere else. They also learned about the three 'important P's' of pheasant hunting: 'Patience, Persistence, and Pain tolerance'.

My son-in-law was one of those people who I was fortunate enough to have the opportunity to mentor into pheasant hunting. I was lucky enough to see him shoot his first pheasant and watch him develop into a quite good pheasant hunter. When my grandson was born, I specifically remember wondering whether I'd still be able to go pheasant hunting when he was old enough to go. Through some quirk of genetics and successfully dodging numerous 'bullets' fired by my own stupidity, I was. It was December. He was eleven years old. He had shot shotguns at flying targets, taken a 'Hunter Safety' course, and walked along while his dad and I hunted pheasants, but he'd never actually hunted pheasants himself. We were hunting on a public property that was 'supervised youth hunting only'. In other words, his dad and I were walking with him, managing the dogs, while he was actually hunting carrying a 20-gauge CZ Ultralight over and under shotgun. We didn't see much at first. The dogs flushed a hen or two. We proceeded through the tall grass to a deep, and steep-sided, drainage ditch. The ground was frozen, and it was difficult to get sufficient traction as we slid into the ditch, crossed the ice in the bottom, and struggled up the other side. We walked just a short distance when a rooster jumped up to the right of my grandson. He shot. Twice. And missed both times. I was ecstatic. The first time most people have a shot at a pheasant they stand there dumbfounded and never shoot at all. My grandson was, understandably, disappointed, but I told him what a great job he had done. We walked around some more and crossed the drainage ditch again. The afternoon was waning, and we were walking with the setting Sun shining off our left shoulders. Suddenly, surprisingly, just as it always is, a brightly colored rooster leaped up into the afternoon sunlight on my grandson's right and flew in front of him to his left. The gun spoke and the rooster dropped into very thick grass. Before we could even get over our surprise at this turn of events or begin to worry about whether we'd find the rooster in the thick grass, my one-year-old lab puppy came bouncing back with the rooster in her mouth. My grandson was a 'pheasant hunter', and I had been there to witness it. There's not a straight line between that ruffed grouse I shot in the coulee country of Wisconsin and my grandson's first pheasant, but if you had enough patience, you could connect the dots.

# Mushrooms

*There's a fine line between morel hunting and just standing in the woods like an idiot.*

Anonymous

I had heard whispers about 'morel mushrooms' (*Morchella esculenta*) for much of my life, but I had only ever found three. They were quite small, and they were growing up through a crack in the sidewalk as I was walking my paper route. I took them home and fried them in butter. People were not wrong – morels are very tasty. I wouldn't find any more for many years, at least in part because I didn't take the time to look for them.

As my biological education continued, both in and out of school, I came to realize that morels aren't actually 'mushrooms' at all. Mushrooms are one type (of several) of reproductive structure produced by 'club fungi' (members of Phylum Basidiomycota), while morels are members of a large group of fungi called 'sac fungi' (members of Phylum Ascomycota). Common names can be deceiving. The tasty morel is actually a type of reproductive structure called an 'ascocarp'. Whether you called them 'mushrooms' or 'ascocarps', I still hadn't learned much about how to find them. Doing so required a 'mushroom mentor' and a greater understanding of fungal biology.

A graduate school friend took me on my first successful morel hunt. He talked about 'blindfolding' me on the drive to his spot, but in the end he relented. What I learned was that morels were only present during a short window of time in late spring, they were well camouflaged, you had to walk around a lot, and it was a good idea to check carefully around dying American elms (*Ulmus americana*). I also learned that morel hunters were VERY protective of spots in which they have found morels. Distinguishing any random dead, or dying, tree from a dying elm turns out not to be trivial. With no, or only very young leaves present, even distinguishing a live elm from other trees can be a challenge. Careful observation of tree bark and branching patterns is essential, and sometimes you're still not sure. And, even if it was a dying, or recently dead elm, there's no guarantee that morels will be present around it. Though they might be two days later. Hence the 'lots of walking' part. Why dying elms? That requires a greater understanding of fungal biology.

Some fungi make their living by decaying dead organisms. Mold growing on forgotten strawberries in your refrigerator is a good example. Some fungi make their living by decaying portions of other living organisms. 'Athlete's Foot' (various species of fungi, e.g., *Trichophyton rubrum*) is an unpleasant example. Other fungi take a more 'cooperative' approach. Lichens are composed of fungi that provide a suitable 'habitat' for photosynthetic algae, more or less 'farming' the algae. The fungus acquires about half of the food that the alga produces through photosynthesis. Morels take a similar approach. Morels (like many other species of fungi) are 'mycorrhizal'. This means that the fungus forms very intimate connections with cells in the roots of the plants. The fungus with its vast network of cells spreading throughout the soil provides the plant with needed mineral nutrients and the plant provides the fungus with some of the food it produces through photosynthesis. It's a good deal for both species. Which species of plant a particular fungus can form a mycorrhizal relationship with is, at least, somewhat species specific. One of the tree species that morels can form a mycorrhizal relationship with is the American elm.

Why were dying elms common enough to walk around in the woods and regularly find? That involves a few other species of fungus, the most virulent of which is *Ophiostoma novo-ulmi*. This, and other closely related species, cause a condition that is called 'Dutch Elm Disease' and is typically fatal to the tree. The disease-causing fungus is not from the Netherlands, it's from Asia, but the initial research describing the disease was done in the Netherlands. Many millions of elm trees have been killed across North America by this disease. From the perspective of the morel fungus associated with an individual elm tree that is dying of Dutch Elm Disease, this is the equivalent of the last grocery store in the area closing. Time to move on. Hence, the production of reproductive structures (ascocarps), each capable of producing many millions of spores, that we try to find, harvest, cook, and eat. Gleefully killing millions of morel babies.

I took my children morel hunting many times. Often it was quite warm in the spring sunshine, and we found ourselves both hot and thirsty. We frequently encountered a particularly unfriendly, and non-native, species in the Iowa woodlands, multiflora rose (*Rosa multiflora*), also known as 'baby rose', 'Japanese rose', 'many flowered rose', 'seven sisters rose', and 'rambler rose'. No matter what you call it, it is an annoying viney shrub with very sharp and recurved prickles. Large patches are literally impassable. This species was intentionally introduced from Asia and has done far too well here. The combination of warm temperatures and short sleeves led to numerous, and bleeding, scratches on arms and faces. My daughter became quite good at spotting morels. My son could walk past a clump of ten and never notice them at all. He was, however, very skilled at eating them.

My daughter had a friend in high school who had eaten morels at our place and wanted to learn how to find them. So, of course, we offered to take her with us, no blindfold required. The day started warm and humid. We walked in a pleasant cool breeze along a ridgetop and then descended into a valley without a breath of wind. We found lots of multiflora rose brambles, and plenty of trees that we thought might have been dying elms, but we found zero morels. We stopped to rest in the shade and eat a sandwich for lunch. My daughter endeavored to keep her friend's spirits up by saying 'my dad almost always finds morels; we just need to keep looking'. No pressure. I was less sure. It's called 'hunting' not 'getting' for a reason.

The weather was rapidly changing. The sky clouded over, and the temperature fell quickly. A light drizzle started to dampen our clothing. We had continued to find nothing, well, no morels. There's always something to see in the natural world. We saw a deer (*Odocoileus virginianus*) run off through the woods and heard a tom turkey (*Meleagris gallopavo*) gobbling in the distance. We left the valley and headed back up the ridge, which seemed to have gotten considerably steeper with the passing of the day. We topped the ridge and reached the trail. We were getting chilly, and the light was getting dim under the cloudy sky. My ever-optimistic daughter suggested that we look at least a little on the other side of the ridge, but none of us wanted to go all the way downhill into the bottom of the next valley. We started giving up some hard-earned elevation, when under a patch of multiflora rose, we saw our first morels of the day. I crawled under the branches to pick them and looked around. There were morels everywhere! The level of excitement and elation is hard to describe. 'This is great' doesn't really cover it. We ended up picking two hundred and sixty-five morels. We struggled to find, amongst our gear, sufficient packs and bags to hold them all. It was chilly, drizzling, rapidly getting dark, and we had a walk of more than a mile back to the vehicle. We didn't care. It's always a good day when you find morels.

Years of morel hunting followed some with great success, some not. The vagaries of weather and timing made for successful, happy, celebrations some years, and made less successful years disappointing, but not surprising. Near the end of my career as a professional biologist, I was fortunate enough to have a graduate student who shared my interest in lichens, and who knew a lot about foraging for wild mushrooms. Given the wide range of toxic chemicals produced by some fungi, I had not dared to extend my fungal foraging beyond morels, which are virtually impossible to mistake for anything else. There is a group of species called 'false morels' (members of the Genus *Gyromitra*), but, in my opinion, they look very little like an actual morel. My graduate student introduced me to several, safe and tasty, fungal species that can be found in Iowa's woodlands. Golden oyster mushrooms (*Pleurotus citrinopileatus*), chicken-of-the-woods (*Laetiporus sulphureus*), and chanterelle mushrooms (members of the Genus *Cantharellus*) have all found their way to my dinner table thanks to her instruction. It's great to have the opportunity to learn from someone who is paying to learn from you.

# The Navy

*The trash and litter of nature disappears into the ground with the passing of each year, but man's litter has more permanence.*

John Steinbeck

I had hiked, with my children, exploring the trails along our local river, the South Skunk, many times before I came to understand that it was home to smallmouth bass (*Micropterus dolomieu*). This portion of the river was well upstream in its watershed and was similar in size to the creek of my youth in which I had trapped my one, and only, beaver. I hadn't done much fishing for many years, but I was interested in revisiting this earlier-in-life passion. Trying to catch a smallmouth bass, which I had not previously done, seemed like a good opportunity.

On a sultry summer Saturday my daughter and I stepped into the river, wearing shorts and old shoes, and started wading upstream. The cool water felt great in the heat. I don't remember what type of lure I was fishing with, but it was garnering zero interest from the smallmouth that were, supposedly, present in the river. In desperation, we used the bug net my daughter had insisted on bringing along to catch a few small minnows in the shallow dead-end bay of a sandbar. I added a minnow to my lure and started casting into areas where the water was deeper. Wham! A fish hit the minnow, and I thought that I'd hooked a fish of considerable size. Once reeled in, however, it was revealed to be a smallmouth bass of eight or so inches in length. Smallmouth bass are quite pugnacious. So began an 'obsession' that spanned many years and resulted in many hundreds of 'smallies' being brought to hand and then released. Only one fish ever made it home from the river for dinner. My obsession spilled over to friends and family members, who, at the slightest indication of interest, were given intensive, and immersive, lessons in the art of stream smallie fishing.

Due to the vagaries of schedules and levels of interest, I frequently found myself fishing for smallies with only the river itself for company. Wading around in the river and walking over sandbars for miles had revealed the presence of shockingly large quantities of human-generated trash. Empty beer cans, lengths of fishing line, plastic bottles, old tennis shoes, etc. Because I found such trash to be an affront to me and disrespectful to the river itself, I had taken to picking up such items, removing my pack, and adding the trash to my load of fishing gear and water. One cool early fall Saturday afternoon, on a stretch of the river that was less familiar to me, I rounded a bend and glanced upstream toward a sandbar. There was something large and white partially buried in the sand. Closer inspection revealed the presence of a cast iron, claw foot, bathtub upside down and partially buried. My first thought was 'well – that's not going to fit in my backpack'. Another thought, however, immediately replaced that initial thought. I had been pondering how to provide our in-coming biology students with an experience that would build camaraderie, connect them to local biodiversity as they were learning about global biodiversity in their first semester introductory class, and provide them an opportunity to provide a service to their new local community. A rare flash of inspiration blazed through my mind. A group of students and a canoe could dig out and remove that bathtub.

About a year later, the first 'trash patrol' of what became called the 'Skunk River Navy' left port and headed downstream toward the sandbar with the bathtub. Our fleet consisted of ten canoes and about fifteen student volunteers. The students were not in the canoes, they were wading in the river, towing the canoes, picking up trash of various kinds, and tossing it into the canoes. I was rather amazed at just how much more trash one could find when one was not focused on fishing for smallies. When we reached the sandbar with the bathtub, I handed shovels to two likely-looking students and told them to 'start digging'. The rest of the students stood around watching and told me there was no reason to dig out the bathtub because it would definitely sink any canoe it was placed in. Clearly, they had far too little experience with canoes. The bathtub was floated out and its shadow never darkened the river again.

The first Skunk River Navy addressed well the camaraderie and community service aspects of my vision, but it did not address the biodiversity component. Benthic macroinvertebrate monitoring was quickly incorporated as a feasible solution to that oversight. Most of the students were from Iowa, or nearby, and had driven on bridges over local rivers and streams many times in their lives without any idea that something besides a few fish might live in them. They had, literally, never met the neighbors. Turning over rocks and using a few nets, forceps, and magnifying glasses fixed that. Skunk River Navy volunteers had up close and personal interactions with damselfly and dragonfly larvae (members of Order Odanata), mayfly larvae (members of Order Ephemoptera), dobsonfly larvae ('hellgrammites'; members of Order Megaloptera) flatworms (members of Order Tricladida), leeches (members of Class Clitellata), crayfish (members of Order Decapoda), and freshwater mussels (members of Class Bivalvia). Less predictably encountered were various aquatic and semi-aquatic vertebrate species including: snapping turtles (*Chelydra serpentina*), green frogs (*Lithobates clamitans*), western fox snakes (*Pantherophis ramspotti*), belted kingfishers (*Megaceryle alcyon*), great blue herons

(*Ardea herodias*), and, on only one occasion, a smallmouth bass that jumped out of the river and landed, to the surprise of everyone involved, in a canoe. Student volunteers emerged from the river, wet, muddy, and tired, but also much better informed about who lived in their neighborhood.

In subsequent years the 'to do list' for 'the navy' became better standardized. Collect from storage the 'tools of the trade': shovels, pickaxe, sledgehammer, tow chain, bolt cutters, saws, trash bags, etc. Assemble the materials required for benthic macroinvertebrate monitoring. Pick up rented canoes, stacked on their trailer, and set up people transportation with the local bus service. Purchase cases of bottled water. Arrange for discount pizzas to be delivered at the intersection of 'gravel road X and the Skunk River'. Work with the Resource Recovery Center to place a roll-off dumpster at the take-out point, which also enabled subsequent weighing of the trash collected during each trash patrol. Check the weather forecast. Check the water level in the river. Re-check the water level in the river. Try to sleep the night before the appointed day.

Each Skunk River Navy trash patrol began with an orientation in a classroom focused on what the volunteers should expect for the day – and an invitation to go back home if that sounded like something they had no interest in. Then the volunteers, sometimes over a hundred, loaded onto buses, or into private vehicles, for the drive to the launch point on the river. Non-student friends and colleagues helped guide the students to the river and shuttled vehicles to the downstream take-out point. Students who had been on previous trash patrols, and were returning to help, unloaded and organized the canoes and gear needed for the day. The students were divided into groups for the benthic macroinvertebrate survey. As the students first entered the river there was, in unison, a group squeal, the pitch of which revealed how chilly the water was that morning. As legs and feet went numb, the squeal was replaced with exclamations of 'eewww!' and 'cool!' as various macroinvertebrates were discovered. After discussion of what had been found, and what that revealed about the water quality (not high) of the river, it was time to turn to the business of trash removal.

On one specific trash patrol day, one of the fifty-one total trash patrols carried out by the Skunk River Navy, it started raining while we were finishing the macroinvertebrate survey. The students were concerned, but we assured them that they would soon be soaking wet anyway, so it didn't really matter. Small groups of students nucleated around each of the ten canoes and the fleet began to work its way downstream starting the approximately three-mile trek to our take-out point. Small trash (beer cans, fishing bait containers, plastic bags, etc.) began to fill our trash bags. A discarded lawn chair, partially buried in mud, was the first piece of 'trophy trash'. The rain stopped and the Sun came out from behind the clouds. The air temperature started to rise and the cool water in the river started to feel good. Large tangles of barbed wire fence, some still attached to metal fence posts, were removed using bolt cutters. Half-buried tires started to show up with some regularity. Each required some digging, tugging, and the washing out of sand and sediment before it went into a canoe. A mysterious object with metal 'pipes' turned out to be a full-sized wooden picnic table buried upside down in the river. This required some effort with shovels to free it from the mud, and then many group members pulling together on the tow chain to pull it up and turn it right side up. Far too big to fit in a single canoe, but not a problem - time to fashion a 'canoe-a-maran'. Two canoes placed side by side, metal fence posts, found in the river further upstream, laid across the two canoes over thwarts. The fence posts were tightly tied to the thwarts and the picnic table, upside down again, was lifted on top. A few tires were added for 'ballast' and it was back to floating downstream. The appearance of a bridge around the next bend, and the presence of a bemused-looking pizza delivery person, signaled that it was time for lunch on a sandbar. It was amazing how quickly 30 large pizzas could disappear. The pizza boxes were added to our trash pile. Students began asking 'how much further?', to which we would reply, 'don't worry, it's all downhill from here'. Some of the students would eventually figure out that we'd been 'going downhill' the whole time. That's just the way rivers work.

Tires, tires, and more tires. The tires were piled high in every canoe, under and over the other trash. The picnic table was festooned with tires. The canoes were full and, not infrequently, dragging on the sandy bottom of the river. The word went out to the entire fleet 'stop picking up trash – we've got all we can handle'. It was sad to wade by more trash and not be able to remove it. The afternoon Sun was warm and was beginning to sink into the western sky when we rounded the last bend and could see the take-out point. Everyone's shoes were packed with sand, leaving far too little room for toes. Muddy hands, muddy shirts, muddy faces, and tired legs, but we had arrived. We now faced another problem – getting the trash from the canoes to the dumpster on the top of the riverbank in the gravel parking lot. The students, and other volunteers, were lined up from the river to the dumpster. Heavily loaded trash bags, tires, etc., were passed up the line one by one. We counted ninety tires. A group of eight brought up the picnic table last of all. The canoes were loaded onto the trailer, and we headed back to campus.

While the morning ride could be characterized as a very quiet 'what did I get myself into' event, the return ride was tired, wet, and raucous. Turning into the parking lot that was our assembly point the students were greeted with a wonderful surprise. My wife and her friends had spent the day baking many dozens of cookies, of a wide range of types. The students attacked the offerings with the enthusiasm of people who had been working hard under challenging conditions all day, while laughing with their new-found friends and telling anecdotes about the day. Slowly the group dispersed, never to be all together again, though some students (not many) would want to return to help us next year. My friends, colleagues, and I would retire to hot showers and adult beverages and reflect upon how we'd managed to 'survive' another Navy.

For twenty years the Skunk River Navy plied the murky waters of the river, and some of its smaller tributaries. In total over eighty tons of trash (everything from lost 'flip flops' to washing machines to port-a-potties to front end loader tires) was removed to a more appropriate location and the daily routines of many benthic macroinvertebrates were briefly interrupted. Because of one beautiful, shining, and hard fighting species, the smallmouth bass, the lives of well over two thousand volunteers had been impacted, hopefully positively. Knowledge of neighboring biodiversity, sometimes deprecated as being akin to 'stamp collecting', can, actually, have meaningful results. Hopefully, none of the Skunk River Navy veterans have ever left an empty beer can floating in a river.

# The Lichen in Winter

*Only those who will risk going too far can possibly find out how far one can go*

                                    T.S. Elliot

We were fifteen years old. A long list of things seemed like a 'good idea' to us. The school break between Christmas and New Year's seemed like a great time to go camping. Besides, if we wanted to grow up to be 'mountain men of the old west', we definitely needed to know how to spend winters camping in the snow. This explained our battered trapping backpacks being stuffed with cotton sleeping bags, canvas pup tents, several boxes of matches, various canned foods, and probably some extra clothes. It was snowing lightly as we left my house and started walking toward our favorite wooded area a few miles away. The snow was accumulating on the tree branches, and soon to the depth of a few inches on the forest floor, as we walked uphill into the woods. We knew a spot that had an open view of the river valley farther up the hill and we thought that would be a great place to set up camp. We hadn't factored in the possibility of wind.

By late afternoon we had the tents set up, the fire started, dinner was burning, the sky was clearing, and the temperature was dropping. We ate something unidentifiable for dinner and huddled closer and closer to the fire, with the woodsmoke stinging our eyes, as the wind began to rise, and the tree branches began dancing above us.

The stars were already bright in the night sky, but it was still early in the evening being so close to the winter solstice. We decided it was time to crawl into our sleeping bags anyway. It was a long night. We learned later that the temperature had reached an overnight low of plus 7 degrees Fahrenheit. My feet were kept pretty warm because I stuffed my small female beagle, who had been given no choice about joining us, into the bottom of my sleeping bag. She didn't complain. My friend wasn't so lucky. By morning he told us his feet were hurting pretty badly, and he didn't want to hike around exploring with us, he'd rather just sit around by the fire. My other friend and I were gone much of the day checking out potential trapping locations for 'next season'. We spent another night in camp before deciding there might actually be something wrong with our friend's feet and packing up to walk back home that morning. My friend, of course, had mild frostbite on both feet. No toes were lost, but his mother wouldn't let him go winter camping with us ever again. Was it a good idea? Well, no one had died and only one third of us had suffered frostbite.

So began a 'winter camping career' that lasted over forty years. It didn't take long before we realized two things: 1) Iowa's winters were too short and too warm; and 2) we needed MUCH better gear. We explored, and camped in, a number of possible locations before we learned about the Boundary Waters/Quetico area of northern Minnesota and southwestern Ontario. We had found the ideal winter camping destination for us. We even convinced ourselves that 'BWCA'. (Boundary Waters Canoe Area) actually stood for 'Big Winter Camping Area'. As is probably obvious, any idiot can be cold in the cold, the trick is being warm in the cold. We spent a lot of time learning how to be warm in the cold. Wool (not cotton!). Moisture-wicking base layers. Wind-proof shell layers. The fact that gaiters are much more than a 'fashion statement'. Synthetic-fill winter weight sleeping bags. Reliable methods for starting fires, even in difficult conditions. How to start backpacking stoves in cold weather conditions to melt snow and provide warm drinks and soups. Settling upon a mutually acceptable high calorie diet that was relatively easy to prepare in the wild and as lightweight as possible. It was a process punctuated by numb fingers, frost-nipped noses, and considerable shivering. We also had to learn effective travel methods. Snowshoes and cross-country skis, and the conditions in which each worked best. The importance of having 'climbing skins' for the skis. The value of having your lightweight shell mittens securely attached to your body when you were traveling in the open out on a windswept lake. The realization that hauling bulky winter camping gear and food on sleds was much more efficient than using a backpack.

My friend who did NOT frostbite his feet on that first winter trip and I went on many winter camping trips with a range of friends, relatives, and acquaintances. Although there was, generally speaking, plenty of misery to go around, we only had to end one trip early to evacuate a companion. A mutual friend pretty seriously frostbit several toes. His wife never let him go winter camping with us again even though no toes were lost. But, of course, schedules and responsibilities changed over time, and that led to a year in which the only people available to go were myself and my son who had a fortunately timed break in his medical school studies. By this point in time, my son was a veteran of several winter camping trips, having started his career with an overnight winter trip at age eight. I had no concerns about taking a trip with just the two of us. I'd been on several trips with just one companion, and I was, quite accurately, confident in my son's abilities as a winter camper.

We drove through the night to reach the Big Winter Camping Area because time was short for both of us, and we wanted as much time as possible in the winter wilderness. After the long drive getting the sleds set up for travel and pulling them across the first couple of lakes, connected by portage trails, was carried out in a bit of 'mental fog'. That meshed well with the cloudy skies and very light freezing drizzle that greeted us. We reached our destination for the night, ate a freeze-dried dinner, and wormed our way into our sleeping bags which had been stuffed inside 'bivy sacks' to avoid the chore of setting up a tent. The morning dawned clear and chilly; it was minus 16 degrees Fahrenheit. Brisk, but quite effective at encouraging a quick breakfast and rapid re-packing of the sleds. The snow squeaked under our ski boots as we made final preparations, clipped into our ski bindings and started breaking trail through knee deep powder snow to the next lake. That warmed us up nicely. The next lake had a couple of long winding channels we needed to pass through, but what was occupying our mind was the next portage. It was longer than the previous portages, rocky, and quite steep in a couple of places. After considerable effort, and cursing, we were both sweated up and removing layers (AKA: 'delaminating'). We were also less than halfway across the portage, but we had climbed to the highest point, and it was 'all downhill from here'. It seemed clear that we would, indeed, make it to the lake we wanted to set up our base camp on.

Upon arrival we searched carefully for a suitable campsite. We needed some flat ground sheltered from the windy lake shore by a band of coniferous trees for the fire pit/kitchen. Previous experience had convinced us that if a campsite 'had a view' it was best to go someplace else. A south-facing exposure, that would have some sunlight much of the day and be sheltered from cold northerly winds, would be nice. Another flat spot to set up a tent. A ready supply of small, dead, standing, trees that would make good firewood. We found a spot that checked all the boxes and set about making our camp. Snow was shoveled to make a spot for the fire and piled up into benches to serve as both seats and a 'kitchen' once the packed snow hardened through the process of 'sintering'. A tent platform was packed in the snow and allowed to sinter for a bit before setting up the tent and putting in sleeping pads, sleeping bags, and other nighttime items. Trails were snowshoed to all the portions of the camp to make for easy travel without needing snowshoes or skis. A readily observed tree branch was chosen to hold the maximum-minimum thermometer so we would know how cold it had gotten overnight. 'Parking spots' were chosen for the sleds so that food and extra gear could be easily accessed when needed. As the sun was beginning to sink toward the horizon, it was time to search for firewood.

Northern Minnesota was not my 'local neighborhood', but it was still important to know the neighbors, especially when it came to firewood. Paper birch (*Betula papyifera*) makes great firewood IF it has been split and allowed to dry for a year or two. A standing dead paper birch tree makes terrible firewood for the same reason that paper birch bark makes good canoes. The bark is effectively waterproof and wood from standing dead paper birch trees works better as a fire retardant than as firewood. Balsam fir (*Abies balsamea*) burns well, but it burns very quickly and makes lots of sparks. Black spruce (*Picea mariana*) is a better choice. But the best southern boreal forest firewood choices are probably white cedar (*Thuja occidentalis*), black ash (*Fraxinus nigra*), and tamarack (*Larix laricina*). White pine (*Pinus strobus*), red pine (*Pinus resinosa*), and jack pine (*Pinus banksiana*) aren't bad either, but they burn pretty fast. The point is that if you're going to go to all the work of cutting it down, dragging it back to camp, and sawing it up into firewood-sized pieces, it makes the most sense to choose trees that will produce good fires. Which, of course, means one has to know how to identify these trees, without using their leaves because deciduous trees (paper birch, black ash, and tamarack) drop their leaves in the fall and dead 'evergreens' (all the rest) no longer have leaves. Soon the fire was crackling, sending out waves of welcome heat, and we were eating chicken Cup-A-Soup fortified with a tablespoon of butter and Minute Rice before the main course of a freeze-dried dinner.

The weather had been forecast to warm up. It didn't. The next morning it was minus 28 degrees Fahrenheit. A quick morning fire, oatmeal, coffee, bacon, and bread fried in butter got us started for the day. We watched black-capped chickadees (*Poecile atricapillus*) and Gray Jays (*Perisoreus canadensis*) flit around camp, hoping to find an overlooked peanut, and wondered how such little creatures were able to survive such cold temperatures with no extra layers. We put food, water, and extra layers into our daypacks. We put on our wind shells, ski boots (pre-cooled overnight), and gaiters, and clipped into our ski bindings. Time to explore. The sky was cloudless, and the bright Sun reflected off the expanse of snow on the lake. We came to the outflow of the lake where there was some open water flowing rapidly over some rocks and spotted the characteristic 'sliding on its belly' track of a river otter (*Lontra canadensis*) in the snow near the water. We detoured, carefully, around the open water to reach the portage trail. A set of tracks revealed that a pine marten (*Martes martes*) had used the portage trail sometime before we did. A red pine squirrel (*Tamiasciurus hudsonicus*) barked angrily at us for disturbing the solitude of the trail. We continued into another lake and saw the tracks of a moose (*Alces alces*) that had been trotting along the seam between lake and forest, stopping to browse on red osier dogwood (*Cornus sericea*) twigs every now and then. We headed back to camp. Our dinner was eaten as the almost full moon began to shine brightly through the trees.

The snow squeaked loudly as I walked on the trail from our tent to the fire pit-kitchen the next morning. The trail passed, conveniently, right by the thermometer, which was easily readable in the early morning light. It was currently at the overnight low of 38 degrees below zero Fahrenheit. I pulled the hood of my parka up over my wool balaclava and set about getting the stove started for breakfast. I heard my son walking on the snow well before I saw him. He stopped to look at the thermometer. Then he announced, "if it gets to minus 40, we're going home!" I did not bother to disagree with him – he hadn't had any coffee yet. By the time we'd finished breakfast, the sunny skies had warmed the air temperature up to minus 25 and we agreed it would be a good day for a day trip. Clear skies, virtually no wind, and a full moon in case it took longer to get back to camp than planned. We packed up our gear and left camp. We started out on the same trail we had made the day before but soon turned to take a portage trail to a lake we'd not been on previously. A gray wolf (*Canis lupus*) pack had preceded us down the trail. A large pile of hair-filled scat confirmed what the tracks had already told us. You have to admire a species that can live in this country year-round and catch all of the food it needs using its legs and teeth.

We had a great day and went a long way. As the sun was getting close to setting, we were at our farthest point, several miles from camp. This likely wouldn't have presented much of a problem, with a full moon soon to rise, even though it was a bit chilly. But, right near the end of the day we encountered the bane of lake country winter campers. Slush (also called 'overflow') under deep snow. It's virtually undetectable until you ski into it. Then you find yourself in ice water up past your ankles, snow above that, and good hard ice beneath your skis. The real problem doesn't arise until you ski out of the slush into dry snow, which promptly balls up and starts to freeze on your skis. Time to take your skis off and scrape them clean before the wet snow freezes solid. We'd encountered slush many times, although we never came to enjoy it. We weren't especially concerned and in the waning daylight, we started heading back toward camp, running into a couple more pockets of slush along the way. The first portage was fairly flat, and we were able to ski across it to the large lake on the far side. The view on the big lake was breathtaking. Bright moon, vast expanse of white snow, fluffy flecks of snow drifting out of an almost completely clear sky, dark trees on the far shoreline. We skied for two miles in a winter wonderland. The upcoming portage, however, was quite steep and rocky necessitating a stop to remove your skis and walk up just wearing ski boots. I was wearing a headlamp, but my vision was partially obscured by the foggy plumes of my breath in the beam of light. I tried and failed to release my ski bindings. Thinking I hadn't done it correctly in the poor light, I tried several more times. Finally, it dawned on me that the slush had gotten into my ski binding release and had frozen it solid in the well below zero temperatures. I could not ski up the steep portage. I could not take my skis off. Clearly, the next logical step was to remove my gaiters, take my ski boots off, carry my skis over my shoulder, with the boots still attached, and walk up the steep portage trail in my socks. There wasn't an ideal amount of traction, but it worked on that portage, and several more, as we headed back to camp. On one of those trails a ruffed grouse (*Bonasa umbellus*), doubtless quite unhappy with us, blasted up out of the snow between the tips of my son's skis. Hard to say who was more surprised, but I'd put my money on my son. Once back at camp, we checked the thermometer and noted that the high temperature for the day had been about minus 15 degrees Fahrenheit. The temperature was now approaching minus 30. We started the stove, heated some water, warmed up our flask of whisky in the warm water to avoid frostbitten tongues, poured some whisky into two cups, and talked about what a great day trip it had been.

The next day was our last of the trip and we stayed close to camp. At one point I was made aware that the time had come to 'answer the call of nature'. Wandering off into the woods seeking a suitable tree to lean against for the somewhat delicate maneuver requires careful attention to detail. It's nice to find a spot that's in the Sun and out of the wind, but it's essential to find a strong tree with very little likelihood of falling over when leaned against. I found such a tree and accomplished the task, but in doing so I noticed something unfamiliar on the bark of the tree across from me. Upon closer inspection I realized I was correct – it was unfamiliar. Relatively large, and green, leaf-like growths with a broadly toothed margin. An oddly sculpted lower surface that was tan in color. I didn't even know what general type of organism it was. A liverwort? A type of parasitic fungus? An epiphytic plant? I grabbed some and put it into the front pocket of my parka.

I was back home and could once again feel the tips of most of my fingers and all of my toes. The skin was nearly finished peeling off my frost-nipped nose. While unpacking I had found the mystery organism stuffed inside the front pocket of my parka. I brought it with me to show to a colleague who I thought might have some idea of what it was. I started to explain where I had found it and she said "Oh – that's an old friend, *Lobaria pulmonaria* (also called 'lungwort'), it's a large and beautiful lichen." A lichen! Why hadn't I thought of that? Turns out that, like virtually every person on Earth, my education in the topic of lichens had been sadly neglected. Return trips to the Boundary Waters led to frequent sightings of lungwort. Just like knowing a person's name makes you far more likely to notice them when you see them, knowing the name of this lichen brought it to my attention frequently. I never, however, saw it in Iowa woodlands and assumed it was an exclusively boreal forest species.

Knowing the name *Lobaria pulmonaria* brought another oversight to my attention. Although I was well-versed in the identity of many of the species that I shared Iowa's natural places with, I knew virtually nothing about lichens in Iowa. This seemed to be a situation that should be rectified. I started reading about, and observing and collecting, lichens. I began to explore the lichen collection in our herbarium. I took a couple of field classes, taught by real lichenologists, on how to identify lichens. Slowly, I came to understand that, although most of Iowa's lichens were rather small and unobtrusive, there was quite a lot of diversity that I, heretofore, had been completely ignorant of. Still, Iowa's lichens were beautiful with the aid of careful observation and a little magnification. I came to be on a 'first name basis' with many of Iowa's lichens including 'star rosette lichen' (*Physica stellaris*) that is very commonly present on tree bark, and the equally common resident of tree bark 'candle flame lichen' (*Candellaria concolor*). I also became familiar with a striking lichen that was called 'goldeneye lichen' (*Teloschistes chrysophthalmus*) and which was common in some parts of the state and virtually absent in other parts of the state. All things considered, coming to know Iowa's lichens was a 'face palm' experience.

I soon came to realize that, like most things involving lichens, our herbarium lichen collection was largely ignored and poorly curated. Packages were falling apart. Labels were nearly unreadable. The scientific names of some lichens had been updated long ago but never corrected in our collection. I, with the help of some students, set about trying to improve the situation. While doing so, I became aware that an older ('deprecated') name for lungwort was *Sticta pulmonaria*, and I had noticed that we had a specimen of this lichen in our herbarium that had been collected in Iowa in the late 1800s. I assumed there had been a misidentification made by a long dead lichenologist and went to find the specimen. I opened the package and there it was. *Lobaria pulmonaria*, without a doubt. I was shocked – northeast Iowa was not in the boreal forest. Further investigation of other lichen collections revealed that lungwort had been collected in Iowa several times in the late 1800s and early 1900s, but no specimens had been collected since. Over the next few years, I, sometimes accompanied by students, walked through over ninety miles of northeast Iowa forests and never found any lungwort, even though it's a large and easily spotted lichen. Like many other more easily noted species, for example, elk (*Cervus canadensis*), black bears (*Ursus americanus*), and gray wolves, it appeared that lungwort had been extirpated from the state not long after settlement by people of European heritage. When you don't know the neighbors, it's easy to overlook them being gone. What caused the loss of lungwort from Iowa's biodiversity is not clear, but at least one Iowan mourns its absence.

My newly acquired interest, and expertise, in lichen diversity led me to decide that, unlike during my education, I was going to provide students with an opportunity to come to know, and love, lichens. I set up a course that provided students with the skills required to identify lichens (and mosses as well) and led them through developing a diversity inventory of lichens for specific field sites. At the end of each semester of the course, the students would present their findings to the landowner, or land manager, of the field site. The landowners/managers were uniformly amazed to learn about the extensive diversity of lichens they had, and had been totally unaware of, on their land. The class would fill each time it was offered and, eventually, a couple hundred students had come to appreciate the wonderful world of lichens. Three of those students went on to do graduate work with me on lichens, earning their master's degrees in the process. Perhaps most important of all, my grandson, at the age of five, became the youngest person in Iowa (to my knowledge) to be able to, almost always, correctly identify something as a 'lichen' or a 'moss'. The consequences of becoming a winter camper played out in many unexpected ways, so I guess it was a 'good idea'.

# Downstream

*To sit down on this bank of sand and watch the river flow.*

Bob Dylan

Iowa has a dearth of publicly accessible land, but it has a lot of usually quite friendly rivers that do not require a great deal of skill to paddle. Sadly, these rivers currently have high levels of nutrients, heavy sediment loads, and far too much human-generated trash. Still, if you're looking for a bit of 'wilderness' in Iowa, a river is your best bet. Legally, Iowa's rivers and streams are classified as 'meandered' or 'non-meandered'. This does not mean what you probably think it means. 'Meandered' rivers are the large rivers with relatively widely spaced bends. 'Non-meandered' rivers (and streams) are smaller and often have frequent twists and turns. I cannot explain the terminology. The legal significance is that State of Iowa owns the riverbed of 'meandered' rivers up to the normal high-water level, while the riverbed of 'non-meandered' rivers is owned by the adjacent landowners. The riverbed, sandbars, etc. of 'meandered' rivers are publicly accessible. You can stand on them without trespassing. Standing on the riverbed of a 'non-meandered' river, without permission of the landowner is, strictly speaking, trespassing here in Iowa. The good news is that the WATER is publicly owned and, as long as you are 'in the act of navigation', you can legally paddle down any river or stream you wish.

I started taking my children hiking when they were quite young and, as quickly as possible, encouraged them to stop thinking that being carried back to our vehicle was an option. We learned our way around many local woodlands, waded shallow creeks, ate snacks on good vantage points, and watched wildlife. We soon ran out of new spots to explore and, as they got a bit older, the pleasant memories of my childhood canoe floats on the Cedar River arose and it became completely clear that I needed to get a canoe. At first, we used borrowed or rented canoes but eventually we purchased a seventeen-foot aluminum canoe that weighed about sixty-five pounds. When we started our canoeing expeditions, my son was just barely big enough to paddle in the bow and my daughter was too small to paddle at all. I got her a small 'toy paddle' so she wouldn't feel left out.

We explored, by canoe, many of our local streams and rivers, but we very quickly identified a favorite river, the Boone River in central Iowa. There's about twenty-five miles of canoeable water before the Boone joins the much larger Des Moines River. The Boone is a non-meandered river, but the river passes through a patchwork of privately-owned and publicly owned land providing sufficient spots to legally stop to rest or eat lunch. The Boone also has, for Iowa, a relatively protected watershed. Steep heavily wooded ridges along the river keep agricultural use well away from the water's edge in most places. The riverbed is mostly sand and rock unlike the muddy, silted in, riverbeds of many of our streams. Freshwater mussels of various species are relatively common. The deeper pools in outside bends of the river are home to smallmouth bass (*Micropterus dolomieu*) and channel catfish (*Ictalurus punctatus*). Although by no means a 'whitewater river', the rate of fall on the river produces strong current and some 'interesting' rocky riffles and small rapids. Clearly, a great place to introduce children to the wonders of floating down rivers in a canoe.

Each canoe trip started with a flurry of activity getting the canoe on a vehicle and the gear organized. Then both my wife and I would drive to the upstream end of our planned trip. We'd leave the canoe there at a public river access and then drive to the downstream takeout point where we'd leave one vehicle. My wife would then drive us back to the canoe and we'd unload our gear for the day. Life vests, waterproof bags with extra clothes and lunch, paddles and anything else we needed were all carried down to the river. We'd get all the gear and people loaded in the canoe, wave goodbye as my wife left to drive home, and head downstream. A palpable sense of peace would descend upon me as soon we rounded the first bend and could no longer see the canoe access. The sound of vehicles on the highway quickly diminished in the distance. The canoe was floating on a sparkling, splashing, highway through a green tunnel of trees. The river was alive with schools of small fish in the shallows and the trails of mussels plowing through the sand. Small branches, with their bark neatly chewed off by beavers (*Castor candensis*), littered the shoreline and the staccato chatter of belted kingfishers (*Megaceryle alcyon*) filled the air. Sometimes we'd see bald eagles (*Haliaeetus leucocephalus*) soaring high above the ridges bordering the river. We'd commonly see great blue herons (*Ardea herodias*) take flight as we approached, and less commonly, we'd see the smaller, and more shy, green herons (*Butorides virescens*) perched on a log along the riverbank.

Occasionally, there would be places where the current noticeably sped up and water splashed around the rocks sticking up above the surface of the river. Careful observation and well-timed paddle strokes were required to navigate the canoe through the riffle, though the canoe grinding to a halt in a shallow spot was a much more likely outcome than a collision with a large rock spilling us into the water. The river was shallow enough that it was rarely 'dangerous', but it certainly focused my attention while carrying such precious cargo. Wearing life vests was absolutely required. We'd begin to pass landmarks named (unofficially) on previous trips. 'Sahara Sandbar'. 'Eagle Rapids'. 'No Way Out Rapids' lived up to its name and we all had to get out and drag the canoe through the shallow water gurgling over slippery algae-covered rocks. After a brief discussion we agreed that stopping for lunch on 'Elbow Sandbar' would be a good idea. Beaching the canoe and tying it to a substantial log so that it wouldn't float away without us, we'd get out lunch and sit on the sand in the summer sunlight to eat it. Usually, we'd bring some cheese and bread to make cheese sandwiches. I only remember one time when the cheese got dropped in the sand and we ate real SANDwiches. After lunch we'd walk around on the sandbar looking at mussel shells, deer tracks, old bones and, if we were lucky, river otters (*Lontra canadensis*) with scat full of fish scales. The kids would play on the large branch of a dead tree that was half buried in the sandbar. They called it 'Old Bowser' for reasons that were never clear to me. Not a cloud in the sky, no one else around, the river quietly flowing past. It felt like wilderness.

Eventually it was time to get back in the canoe. We were now floating over private land in public water. Soon we could hear the water rushing through one of the more dramatic riffles on the river that we referred to as 'Sarn Gebir', thanks to J.R.R. Tolkien. Our version was much less intimidating. The canoe hung up briefly on a limestone ledge, but then it slipped, right side up, into the water below and we continued to head downstream. The Sun was beginning to sink into the west, but the warmth of the day still made it feel good to paddle through shady parts of the river when possible. Sometimes we'd dip our caps into the water and then put them back on to cool ourselves off. The quiet movement of the canoe through the water allowed us to sneak up on a family of otters swimming around in the river. Or maybe they were just unconcerned by the slow, less agile, aluminum behemoth that was headed their way. In any event, we got a great look at them. Some things had gotten better. During my childhood canoe trips there were no otters to see. My children were more fortunate. The canoe ground on the sand once more as we reached the takeout point. Evening was beginning to fall, and the temperatures were dropping a little. Canoe on the vehicle. Gear in the vehicle. Discussion of where we should go next time all the way back home.

# Liquid Water

*The way of a canoe is the way of the wilderness, and of a freedom almost forgotten*

Sigurd Olson

My son and daughter had become pretty good canoeists by taking day trips on our slow moving, muddy, local rivers, and they had been on week-long canoe trips in the Boundary Waters with me. Traveling in the area when the water was liquid was quite surprising to me given my previous winter experiences. Canoes are MUCH more efficient at carrying gear than sleds pulled through snow on frozen lakes. My wife, to be honest, was not an 'outdoors person'. Her idea of an 'adventure' included sitting under a blanket, sipping tea, and reading a romance novel. But she became convinced that she was missing an important part of our children's development as young humans. We decided to take her with us on our summer's expedition to the Boundary Waters, having planned a less challenging trip that only involved one portage over a mile in length. My wife did well, though no one would conclude she was in her 'natural habitat'. We caught northern pike (*Esox lucius*) for dinner one night, and a lake trout (*Salvelinus namaycush*) for dinner another evening. At one point, my wife sat on a sandy beach waiting for the rest of us to finish the second leg of a double portage and concluded she was in the most beautiful place she'd ever seen. She also got to see first-hand that our teenage children were already quite competent in the outdoors, and on the cusp of growing into very capable adults. She still wasn't a fan of the mosquitoes.

Family canoe trips continued for a few years, though my wife eventually 'graduated' to staying in a cabin on the edge of the Boundary Waters. My children and I, sometimes with the company of friends, and later, with their spouses, would take both day trips and shorter multi-day trips knowing we'd come back to a warm welcome and a good dinner. One summer, my son and I had the opportunity to introduce his wife to the Boundary Waters. My daughter-in-law had not had much experience in wilderness settings, but she felt safe being in the company of experienced wilderness adventurers. We paddled, we swam, we fished, and we had lake trout for dinner. It was great to have the chance to share a place I loved with my daughter-in-law. It was late summer and unusually warm and humid. As darkness began to fall, we saw clouds and distant lightning on the horizon. We got into our tents, to escape the mosquitoes. It was so warm I didn't want to be in my sleeping bag, and I struggled to go to sleep but eventually nodded off. At about 3:00 AM I woke up to the wind howling and thunder crashing. I have always enjoyed the feeling of being 'snug' in my tent with a storm raging outside. A couple of thin layers of nylon make an incredible difference. The rain began to pound on the tent and the wind roared. I heard a 'crack' and felt something hit the side of the tent, pushing my left leg towards the center of the tent. I figured a branch had broken off and, blown by the wind, had whacked my tent. The tent wasn't leaking, so 'all good'. The rain and wind died down and I rolled over and went back to sleep. I woke to the sound of my daughter-in-law's rather worried voice saying 'Jim, are you alright?'. I answered in the affirmative and commented that 'we had a nice little storm last night, eh?'. I got dressed and exited the tent and learned what caused the worry in her voice. It wasn't a 'just a branch' it was a whole tree. Not a giant tree, but not tiny either. The main trunk had missed hitting my tent by only a few feet. Just one smaller branch had hit the side of my tent. It was a sobering realization of the risk posed by high winds and trees with shallow root systems due to the thin layer of soil overlying solid bedrock in this part of the world. We learned later that a person in another part of the Boundary Water had been killed during this storm by a tree falling on their tent. Being experienced helps minimize the risks posed by wilderness, but experience does not entirely eliminate risk.

For a number of years, it became typical for me to visit the Boundary Waters both by canoe in the summer and by snowshoes and skis in the winter. Spending time in the southern boreal forest during the snow free part of the year made it clear that while Iowa's lichens tended to be small and subtle, the boreal forest's lichens were large, all over the place, and 'in your face'. I felt a need to make their acquaintance as well and so came to know 'bristly beard lichen' (*Usnea hirta*), 'boreal oakmoss' (*Evernia mesomorpha*), 'rock tripe' (*Umbilicaria mammulata* and its close relatives), 'powdered sunshine lichen' (*Vulpicidia pinastri*) amongst numerous others. The most obvious lichens, because they cover the ground in many places, are the 'reindeer lichens' (various members of the genus *Cladonia*). The boreal forest had a rich diversity of larger, less subtle, lichens that I had snowshoed through, and on, for many years rarely noticing their existence and not knowing any of their names.

A work colleague, knowing of my many trips to the Boundary Waters, asked whether I would like to help him lead a field trip course to the Boundary Waters at the end of each spring semester. I immediately liked the idea, since that would mean even more time spent there. We decided our goals were for students to experience the beauty of southern boreal forest, learn the skills needed for travel and camping in a wilderness area, and to begin to become familiar with the biodiversity of the area. Not surprisingly, I wanted to include meeting the lichen 'neighbors' in the region as well. We would recruit students each fall semester and ended up teaching the course for 15 consecutive years. During the spring semester the students would do some research and give a presentation to the class on some aspect of the biodiversity of the boreal forest. We organized the group gear, tents, water filters, 'aquatic sampling gear' (i.e., fishing poles and lures), cooking supplies, etc., while they organized their personal gear, following our recommendations for an early spring trip in the Boundary Waters. At that time of year, there could still be ice on some of the lakes, and it might even snow a little. After the spring semester officially ended the best part of our semester would begin with a ten-hour drive north.

Each group of students, and each trip, was unique. The weather varied. Our destinations were different. The experience levels and attitudes of group members ranged widely. One year the wind changed direction, and a large forest fire headed in our direction. The Forest Service flew in, landing in the lake, to inform us that we needed to leave by a route we had brought no maps for. But the course curriculum was always the same. The students learned various wilderness skills from paddling a canoe, to filtering water, to camp cooking, to how to saw and split firewood and then light a fire. To encourage the students to focus on the local biodiversity we devised a 'biodiversity bingo' game with categories such as 'vascular plants', 'mammals', 'bryophytes', 'birds', and of course 'lichens'. The students worked in teams to compete for 'prizes' of mini candy bars, which doesn't seem like much until you remember the nearest convenience store was many miles of paddling and portaging away. The competition to find the various organisms on the bingo sheets could be surprisingly fierce. We'd start most days with a breakfast of oatmeal and coffee or tea, followed by a rousing round of biodiversity bingo. The student groups would wander around in the woods, and along the lakeshore, near our base camp looking for organisms on their bingo sheets. I had provided each student with a 'nerd-a-scope' (AKA, a magnifying glass) and a custom-made guidebook with pictures so they could carefully examine lichens and mosses to determine their identity. I would luxuriate in my hammock and student groups would bring me small samples of lichens or mosses, provide me with their putative identification, and I would determine whether they could cross off that species on their bingo sheet. Student groups that had, hopefully, correctly identified a tree, tracks on the shoreline, or scat in the woods required me to rise from my hammock and accompany them to determine whether they were correct. In and amongst eating snacks and gathering firewood, that's how we spent most mornings.

In the afternoon we would often attempt to catch some fish for dinner, though we, of course, also had food that didn't require us catching fish. Crossing off 'northern pike' or 'lake trout' on their bingo sheets required a member of the group to ACTUALLY catch the fish. Almost catching the fish only to have it 'throw the hook' right next to the canoe didn't count, nor did watching members of other groups catch fish. So, the motivation to get in a canoe (first putting on chilly wet boots) was pretty high. Typically, most of the students had not caught fish, or at least not caught fish with teeth like northern pike or lake trout. Mostly, we would paddle our canoes and troll our lures behind our boats. The fishing was great, but the catching was often slow. And then a 'yelp' would arise from a student and their fishing pole would be bent nearly double. Given the 'tooth situation', I would typically be in charge of landing the fish whether it was hooked by a person in my canoe or not. It could be exciting, but I only got a fishhook poked through one of my fingers a few times. If we were successful in inviting a fish or two home for dinner, those students who had caught the fish were invited to participate in a fish filleting lesson. Some declined, but most agreed. I would demonstrate on one side of the fish, and with a very careful eye to safety, hand the fillet knife to the student to do the other side. All of the group would gather round to watch the proceedings. Most of the students had never seen the whole process that had underpinned many of the meals of their life. A living organism in the natural world, captured, killed, cleaned, cooked, and eaten. The food chain in 'up close and personal' action. Once while we were eating our fried fish dinner, we had a beautiful male black and orange Blackburnian warbler (*Setophaga fusca*) land on a branch above us. It was not a species on the bingo sheet, but we all enjoyed its visit.

On each trip we would also set aside days, depending on the weather conditions, to take day trips to nearby destinations, seeking to find, or find evidence, (e.g., tracks) of bingo species along the way. On day trips, a specific group of students would be assigned the task of 'navigation'. Use of a map and compass became another wilderness skill learned, typically, by employing 'trial and error', which often resulted in significant extra paddling. On one trip the weather had been windy and cold, even whipping up a thunderstorm that turned the surface of the lake white with floating hail. We waited until a day with more friendly weather and took a day trip to a rarely visited portion of the Boundary Waters hoping to find hungry lake trout. We were returning, empty handed, back to our camp when we observed a lone individual across a bay wearing a red life jacket and waving their arms frantically. My co-leader and I agreed we needed to stop and see if there were some sort of problem. When I stepped out of my canoe the person, an older gentleman, asked 'are you real?'. I took this to mean that 'yes, there was a problem'. Once I assured him that I was real, he was very happy. In fact, no one has ever been that happy to see me, before or since. It turned out that he had been on an early season solo canoe trip and had lost his canoe, with all his gear and food, on a windy morning, eight days previous. This presented the students with an unplanned, but very clear, lesson on the importance of being careful and well-prepared while in the wilderness. Nature does not care whether you live or die.

We found his canoe a couple miles away floating in a small bay of the lake and took him back to our camp for the night. Not surprisingly he was quite weak and struggled to walk the portages. The next morning the two strongest student paddlers and I took him thirteen miles and nine portages out to the nearest road. I paddled his solo canoe, and he rode in the middle seat of our three-person canoe with the two students paddling. Our evacuee had been overdue by several days and the Forest Service had been actively searching for him. His family was very relieved. After a lunch provided to us by the local outfitter, we turned around and headed back to the rest of our group back at camp. The wind had come up considerably and we were paddling into it. The lake that our camp was on the far side of was rather large and the waves were too big to safely paddle the short route directly to our camp. So, we paddled the long way along the coast, partially sheltered from the wind by some islands, and got back to our camp right as darkness fell. We'd brought back fresh cookies made by the outfitter's kitchen staff, much to the delight of the rest of the group. I crawled into my sleeping bag early and slept soundly that night.

After seven or eight days in the wilderness the students would return home for the summer sunburnt, and bug-bitten, but hopefully with a new set of wilderness skills and a much broader range of familiarity with biodiversity. All of the students who took this field trip class returned home safely with no more damage than a bruise, blisters, or scrapes. Some of the students would contact me later for advice about planning a trip with their friends or family. I was delighted to help and even loaned out some gear on a couple of occasions. If special natural areas don't have people who know, and love, them, they may cease to be special natural areas through the activities of people who do not know and love them. I was honored to have helped develop some people who knew and loved the Boundary Waters.

# Peak Experience

*The mountains are calling and I must go.*

John Muir

We are all born prisoners of gravity. We're not even able to raise our head, let alone stand on our feet. Fighting gravity is a life-long challenge. Perhaps that is why I made friends with another graduate student who I first saw while he was wearing a T-shirt that said, "Fight Gravity." He was, of course, an experienced rock climber. I began to 'learn the ropes' under his tutelage. Use of a belay plate. The figure eight knot. Setting up rappel anchors. Chocks, hexes, and 'Friends'. There was a lot to learn, and failure to learn thoroughly could have severe consequences.

We began to spend a great deal of time together at a nearby state park that had numerous quartzite rock outcrops. The cliffs weren't very tall, but they were plenty tall enough that a fall could cause death or serious injury. I found the threat of 'death or serious injury' to be very effective at taking my mind off of being in graduate school and going more deeply into debt every month. Although buying 'bargain basement' climbing gear still seemed like a bad idea. Because we could walk up the 'easy way' to the top of all the climbing routes, we spent the vast majority of our time 'top roping'. This is an excellent way to learn, and practice, climbing skills because you are connected by a rope to a (hopefully) secure anchor above you. If you were trying to climb a route that exceeded your ability and you slipped off and fell, there was just a brief moment of panic before the rope yanked on your climbing harness and pulled you to a stop. Not dying meant that you could practice the route as many times as you wished.

But top roping is not the way mountains are climbed – at least not the first time. It's not possible to go to the top of a mountain and send a rope all the way down. You have to actually climb the mountain first. We thought we were interested in climbing mountains someday. That requires what is called 'lead climbing'. You climb while pulling the rope up behind you. Along the way you place intermediate anchors, using chocks, hexes, etc., and using a carabiner, clip your rope to the anchor. If you are top roped, you never fall more than a few feet, barely time to enjoy the ride. If you are lead climbing, it's a bit different. If you're five feet above your last anchor, you'll fall ten feet before the rope stops your fall, assuming you put the anchor in properly. If you're ten feet above your last anchor, you'll fall twenty feet before the rope stops your fall. Things get serious quickly. Naturally, we were attracted to lead climbing. The one time I took a serious fall while lead climbing, and ended up gasping on the ground, I did not die nor was I seriously injured. But my right thigh looked a lot like hamburger and my right elbow was bleeding profusely. I was lucky. Gravity is not 'just a good idea, it's the law'.

It was a warm late summer day. The trees in the forest surrounding us were in the process of being defoliated by 'European spongy moth' (*Lymantria dispar*) caterpillars. They were so numerous that, if we listened quietly, we could hear them munching, apparently in unison, on the leaves. As you might guess from the common name, European spongy moths (sometimes called 'gypsy moths'), are not native to North America. But they do really well here and are able to feed on the leaves of over 500 species of North American trees. They are considered to be one the most destructive invasive species worldwide. I took note of the spongy moth infestation, but I was more focused on the 'Weissner Face'. This was a beautiful sheer rock face at the top of a cliff overlooking the lake in the state park far below. I had top roped this climb several times, but on this day, I was planning to lead climb it. The bottom part of the climb was well within my abilities and had numerous good anchor opportunities. The top part was much closer to the upper limit of my abilities and had way fewer anchor opportunities. I clung on to secure holds at the base of the upper part, trying to remember exactly how I had previously climbed that section, before summoning the courage to commit. Reaching the top was a great relief.

Several years later my rock-climbing friend, a friend of his who was a very good climber, and I set out to climb a mountain. We were attempting the easiest 'technical' route on Long's Peak in Colorado. The route is called 'Kiener's Route' and begins with a climb up a snow-covered couloir called the 'Lambslide' that requires the use of crampons. It quickly became clear that I was the 'weak link' in our trio. After reaching the top of the Lambslide, we exited onto 'Broadway Ledge' and removed our crampons. Climbers have quite the sense of humor when it comes to using the word 'broad'. It's barely a foot in width in some places and provides a stunning view of the 2,000 feet high vertical rock wall called the 'Diamond', which makes Long's Peak identifiable from many miles away. After coming to the end of Broadway, we turned uphill and did several pitches of relatively easy (at sea level – I didn't find them to be easy at 13,000 feet above sea level) rock climbing. Finally, we emerged onto the summit (14,259 feet above sea level) of Long's Peak and, gratefully, sat down on a flat rock. Our respite was to be short-lived. Within a few minutes a thunderstorm began to climb up over the peak and we needed to quickly exit the lightning strike zone. We were soon swallowed up in a mixture of dense fog and intermittent hail. Fortunately, our friend knew the route well and successfully guided us to a secure eyebolt in the rock from which we could rappel to a snow field that would allow us access to the hiking trail (the 'Keyhole' trail) that would take us back down the mountain. Rappelling down through thick fog to a white snow field, which was invisible through the fog, was quite effective at keeping my attention focused on whether the rope was long enough.

I was very tired and the ill-fitting mountaineering boots that I had borrowed from a friend had led to numerous blisters on my feet. I could not keep up with my friends and told them I'd be fine, to just wait for me at the parking lot. As mountain weather often does, it changed. The sky cleared and it got much warmer as I descended. It was late in the day, and I was alone on the trail. I looked over to my left at a snowfield and I saw things moving on it. At first, I thought I had reached the 'hallucination stage', but turning away and looking back again led to the same conclusion. There was a group of birds on the snowfield. Amazing. They were 'white-tailed ptarmigan' (*Lagopus leucura*). I had never seen them before, and I have never seen them since. Biodiversity is engaging, even when you're exhausted.

I never participated in another 'technical' mountain climb, even as the 'weakest link'. Although my rock-climbing career came to an end, I continued to occasionally ascend mountains via hiking trails. Many years later I was in Colorado visiting my son and we decided to hike up James Peak (13,271 feet above sea level). Similar to my ascent of Long's Peak, the hike started on a snow field, but it was not steep enough to require crampons. Almost immediately it seemed as though the amount of oxygen in the air was substantially lower than I remembered. It also seemed that gravity had gotten stronger, though I am not aware of any principle of physics that would allow that. We hiked through a wide valley before beginning our ascent up to the peak in earnest. My son paused occasionally to allow me to catch up. My pace slowed in concert with increased elevation and the steepness of the trail. During a pause to catch my breath, something I was doing every twenty-five yards or so, I saw a rather rotund furry animal looking at me. A 'yellow-bellied marmot' (*Marmota flaviventer*), very similar in appearance to the 'woodchucks' (*Marmota monax*) that are common in Iowa. After concluding that, in my condition I was no threat, it took a few steps down the trail toward me before heading off into the rocky alpine tundra on a mission of its own. Blissfully, no thunderstorm appeared after I reached the summit.

After recovering somewhat from oxygen deprivation, I began to look around and take note of all of the amazing lichens covering the rocks at the summit. It is truly incredible that anything, animal, plant, or fungus, can make a living in the extreme environment of a mountain top. Blazing sun with high levels of ultraviolet radiation. Dry conditions. Wind and cold. Not an easy place to make a home. And yet, here they were, and in considerable diversity. I started picking up rocks with various lichens on them and stuffing them into my backpack. As I kept noticing different, and potentially different, lichens, more rocks went into my backpack. Shouldn't be an issue, it was all downhill from here. Fortunately, the majority of the rocks were far too big to fit into my backpack. As we started to head back down the trail, I relearned a lesson I had learned many times before. Going uphill is hard on the lungs. Going downhill is hard on the legs. A backpack full of rocks does not help. Sometimes too much knowledge about lichens, or anything else, can be painful. Eventually, I made it to the bottom with what was later determined to be twenty-five pounds of rocks in my backpack. My son shook his head at my silliness in adding to my load and pointed out that I 'could have left some rocks on the mountain'. But I had wanted to take a closer look at these amazing mountain top lichens before gravity imprisoned me again. In the process I met some cool neighbors that were new to me including 'brown tile lichen' (*Lecidia atrobrunnea*), 'granite-speck rim-lichen' (*Lecanora polytropa*), and 'copper patch lichen' (*Sporastatia testudinea*). It was worth every step.

# More Fishing

*Many men go fishing all of their lives without knowing that it is not fish they are after.*

Henry David Thoreau

Between learning about the smallmouth bass (*Micropterus dolomieu*) swimming in a river a twenty-minute drive from home and learning how to catch various species of fish in the lakes of the southern boreal forest, my interest in fishing was thoroughly revitalized. I was interested in expanding my fishing adventures into new challenges. One of those challenges involved an emblematic fish species of the clear, deep, lakes of the Northwoods: the lake trout (*Salvelinus namaycush*).

During our trips to the Boundary Waters Canoe Area, we had caught numerous lake trout. Their pink to orange-colored flesh was delicious when the fillets were cooked, skin side down, on a cedar plank over a fire. But we'd never caught any 'big' lake trout, just 'average' fish weighing about one to three pounds. We had heard rumors about a nearby lake in which big lake trout could be found and we decided we needed to go there. The problem was that there was no portage trail to (Redacted) Lake, and it was about a half mile of 'bushwhacking' to get there from the nearest lake that did have a portage to it. The bushwhacking involved stomping through a hummock-filled marsh for longer than was fun, going up a steep ridge through thick trees, mostly young balsam firs

(*Abies balsaminea*), and then heading down a long slope choked with deadfall trees, steep rocky ravines, and thickets of speckled alder (*Alnus incana*). Alder bushes grow with numerous stems of similar size, some of which start out more or less horizontal to the ground before curving up toward the Sun. They are great at being trip hazards and at obscuring the vision needed for accurate navigation. I knew all this because I had taken a solo, boat-less, recon trip to (Redacted) Lake. On a subsequent trip up north, I convinced my son-in-law that the two of us, with some reasonable amount of effort, would be able to get a canoe there. I was wrong.

Before my next trip up north, I purchased an inflatable kayak that could be rolled up and carried in a large backpack. After paddling to the closest lake, I reached the shortest point for doing the bush-whack. I stepped out of my solo canoe into the marsh and shouldered the big pack that also included fishing gear, lunch, water, extra layers of clothes, etc. It is very easy to get 'turned around' in dense boreal forest, and I did, but eventually, huffing and puffing on a warm summer day, I was on the shoreline of (Redacted) Lake. The kayak was inflated and I put a large lake trout lure with two sets of large, sharp, treble hooks on my line and boarded the plastic-hulled kayak. What could go wrong? I paddled, trolling with my lure behind the kayak. I changed to other lures of different colors or that sank to different depths. Hours passed. Nothing. Back to the bush-whack and paddling across several lakes to our home (a cabin) for the week. A year passed before another effort was possible. This time my son-in-law came with me as we bush-whacked to (Redacted) Lake. Thankfully, he carried the pack with the kayak. We trolled around the periphery of the lake. We tried different lures. We noticed that we were sinking because there was a slow leak in the hull of the kayak. We came ashore to re-inflate it. We decided we should probably give up and paddle back to the point where we would retrace our steps to the lake that we'd left our canoe on. It only made sense to troll while on the way there. My son-in-law grunted and his pole bent sharply. He said, "I'm not sure what it is, but it's big." Each time he would bring in some line and get the fish closer to the surface, the drag on his reel would scream and the fish would descend back into the depths. Finally, I could see the fish, still quite deep, in the clear water. It was big, and it was a lake trout. As my son-in-law brought the fish closer to the kayak, I could see that it was caught by only one hook through its lower jaw. That left five hooks, each with the potential to tear a hole in the heavy duty, but still plastic, hull of the kayak. It dawned on me then 'what could go wrong'. Without going into any details, I successfully landed the fish without sinking the kayak. It was a beautiful lake trout that weighed well over ten pounds. My son-in-law and I looked at each other and both said "crap – now we have to come back here."

And we did. Numerous times, including a memorable trip that included my son, my daughter, and my son-in-law. By taking turns in the kayak, while I served as the 'trolling motor', all of them managed to catch a large lake trout. We filleted the trout and surrounded the fillets with ice packs for the trip back to the cabin. I managed to get turned around on the way back to our canoes, and we ended up at a sheer cliff being bitten simultaneously by mosquitoes and deer flies. A slight, but annoying, course adjustment and we were back on track. There was, however, still an issue. I loved fishing up north, but only got to do so one or, at most, two weeks each year. I also loved fishing for smallmouth bass at home, but the river was often too high and muddy from rapid run-off of rain through Iowa's dramatically drained and tiled agricultural landscape, to successfully catch smallmouth. I needed another fishing opportunity. I thought back on my childhood and remembered the fun we had catching channel catfish (*Ictalurus punctatus*) and common carp (*Cyprinus carpio*). That's a type of fishing you can almost always do in Iowa, at least when the rivers aren't frozen over. I had some success, but it turned out to be harder than I remembered, or maybe I just didn't remember all the times that we didn't catch fish when we were kids. In any case, my grandson, who by this point in time was very interested in fishing, came to the rescue. He told me that some guy on YouTube was posting videos about catching catfish and carp. I was skeptical, but I humored my grandson because I did not, in any way, wish to diminish his interest in fishing. The guy was using terminal tackle that I'd never heard of. 'Method leads' and 'hair rigs'. They worked really well. It's good to have the opportunity to learn new things from your buddies, even if they are your grandson.

Sometime later, my grandson was staying with us for a week during the summer when his usual childcare was unavailable. This translated to fishing with my grandson every day for a week. It was a hot, humid day, and we were on a river channel upstream from a large reservoir in my boat, an ancient twelve-foot-long V-bottom with a small outboard motor. We were anchored up and fishing downstream of the boat where the current from a larger channel washed over a shallow point and merged with the smaller channel we were in. The method leads and hair rigs were working well, and we were catching channel catfish and carp with some regularity, though most were fairly small. Suddenly, his pole leaped toward the bow of the boat, and when he secured it, the pole bent, and the drag was buzzing as the fish stripped the line off the reel. My grandson tried to get me to help him, but once I was sure that he wouldn't be pulled out of the boat, I told him "no, you can do it, just keep the tip of your pole up and take your time." After a lengthy fight between a young human and a fish, a beautiful and massive common carp surfaced along the starboard side of the boat, and I netted it. My fish scale said it weighed thirteen pounds. My grandson was ecstatic and kept saying 'personal best, personal best' as we slid the fish back into the river. Not long after, I caught a nice fish that I assumed was a carp as well, but when I brought it into the boat, it looked 'funny'. It was definitely not a carp, but

I did not know what it was. My grandson took one look at the fish and said "oh – that's a smallmouth buffalo." (*Ictiobus bubalus*) He'd learned that on YouTube too. You can learn a lot from young people if you listen to them.

# Happy Animals

*Hunting forces a person to endure, to master themselves, even to truly get to know the wild environment. Actually, along the way, hunting and fishing make you fall in love with the natural world.*

Hank Shaw

Years of driving around in the 'wilds of Iowa' had cemented my love of pheasant (*Phasianus colchicus*) hunting and my love of sharing the meat from the pheasants with family and friends. I also enjoyed learning to cook various, and tasty, pheasant dishes. I, like the vast majority of humans who have ever lived, was an 'omnivore'. I ate meat, I ate plants, and I also ate fungi, which, as it turns out, are actually more closely related to animals than plants. This draws into question whether a mushroom pizza is a vegetarian option or not. I also ate lots of bacteria, but that was unintentional, completely unavoidable, and likely essential to a properly functioning microbiome. What is clear is that humans evolved as omnivores. Our teeth and our digestive systems tell the tale of a species evolved to eat both plants and animals. Of course, in the modern world, it is possible to live, and eat only plants, as long as certain supplemental vitamins are also consumed. It's a choice that is possible to make. Animals, however, are going to die anyway. Farm machinery, while plowing, planting, and harvesting, kills innumerable insects, nestling birds, small mammals, snakes, and other creatures. Agricultural chemicals kill both 'target' (pests) and 'non-target' (collateral damage) species. Fertilizer run-off into streams results in 'dead zones' in which low dissolved oxygen levels kill any animals unable to leave the area quickly enough. Trucks carrying grain, or produce, frequently hit and kill white-tailed deer (*Odocoileus virginianus*), cottontail rabbits (*Sylvilagus floridanus*), raccoons (*Procyon lotor*), and opossums (*Didelphis virginiana*) amongst numerous other species. Life causes death.

Unless your cells can carry out photosynthesis (they can't), something is going to die so you can live. It could be a pig (*Sus scrofa*), it could be corn (*Zea mays*) babies (i.e., each corn kernel could, if not killed and eaten, grow into a new corn plant), it could be the reproductive structure ('mushroom') of the 'pizza mushroom' (*Agaricus bisporus*) containing, literally, millions of spores, each capable of growing into a new mushroom. You can choose who is going to die, some other organism, or yourself (i.e., starve to death), but that's it. Different people, based on culture and personal preferences, make different choices. I choose, in agreement with my evolutionary history, to be an omnivore.

I tried to get both of my children interested in pheasant hunting, but they were involved in other activities, and they were less enamored with 'seemingly walking forever and then being terrified by a pheasant flushing close enough to hit your leg with its wing' than I was. I did manage to find some hunting buddies who would join me, on and off, for various numbers of seasons, depending on their age and their level of interest. My dog companions got old, retired from hunting, and then died, while new dog companions came along to learn the mysterious, and deceitful, ways of the ring-necked pheasant. Due to limitations of both time and hunting regulations, it was impossible to bring enough pheasants home to provide meat for my family all year long. So, we bought beef (*Bos tarus*), chicken (*Gallus gallus*), deli turkey (*Meleagris gallopavo*) slices, etc. at the grocery store.

During all of my wandering around Iowa looking for places to hunt pheasants, I was also becoming aware of less pleasant facts. Cattle are living mostly in densely packed open air feedlots. Pigs, chickens, and turkeys are mostly raised in very densely packed 'confined animal feeding operations'. These are most definitely not the sort of conditions in which these animals would naturally live. Although I can tell when my dogs are happy, I'm not sure how to tell whether chickens are happy. But it seems unlikely that any animal living in a confined animal feeding operation is 'happy'. The dense populations are convenient for producers, but can lead to disease outbreaks in the animals, and unavoidably lead to gigantic amounts of manure that are difficult to manage and often cause both air and water pollution. Huge portions of Iowa's land surface are used to grow corn and soybeans (*Glycine max*) to feed all these animals. I was not happy with this state of affairs and began to question whether being an omnivore was an acceptable life choice to me.

As time went on, and family and work responsibilities became less intense, I began to expand my hunting horizons. In part, I wanted to seek new challenges and learn new things about my neighbors. But most importantly, I had decided that although I wanted to eat meat, I wanted, insofar as possible, to eat meat that came from animals who had lived 'happy lives'. The kinds of lives that their species had evolved, over millions of years, to live. I first started with wild turkeys (*Meleagris gallopavo*), which are bigger than pheasants, but a legal limit of, at most, four turkeys per year (two in the spring and two in the fall) made clear that turkeys could not be the complete answer. Especially given that I have never managed to kill four, wily and wary, wild turkeys in a single year. Then I moved on to deer hunting – lots of potential for meat from animals that lived happy lives there. Plus, Iowa has a large population of deer, and they are not quite as wary as wild turkeys. I started deer hunting much later in life than most deer hunters, in part because

I erroneously believed that I didn't like the taste of venison. As it turned out, what I didn't like was the taste of poorly prepared venison. Well prepared venison was great! Next, a student of mine introduced me to waterfowl hunting. I almost immediately regretted not having started waterfowl hunting many years earlier, even though we did not get a single shot opportunity that first day.

I now had several more options available to hunt for dinner, and much to the 'delight' of my wife, the need for more gear, various types of boots, and other tools of the trade. The learning curve was steep, and regular success was well off in the future. I received some help from various hunting buddies along the way and continued to improve my skills at inviting the neighbors 'home for dinner'. My first turkey was called into shotgun range by a friend. My first deer was a small doe shot with a traditional side hammer muzzleloader from a tree stand put up by a friend on his land. Although I had previous experience gutting and skinning animals, butchering a large animal like a deer was a new challenge for me. I got some help with that too. I started getting better at deer and turkey hunting about the time my daughter got married to my son-in-law. He was quite interested in becoming a hunter, and I got to help him shoot both his first deer and his first turkey. We started spending quite a lot of time together and my daughter began to get envious. She also started to reconsider her long-held position of lacking any interest in hunting.

By adulthood both of my children were avid and accomplished outdoors people, which was a source of great joy for me. Neither were hunters. Seeing the fun her husband was having hunting with me, and enjoying the meat that we were bringing home, she decided that she would like to give deer hunting a try herself. She started with the goal of taking a deer with a modern, 'compound', bow. But being a successful bowhunter typically requires a great deal of time, something that a parent of a young child and a person with a demanding professional career, has far too little of. Eventually, she expressed an interest in 'trying out' my muzzleloader. By then I had transitioned to an in-line muzzleloader with a scope. I took her to a gun range, and she tried it. Yes, it was loud, and yes, there was some recoil, but really, it was not all that bad. With this tool she could accurately shoot a deer at one hundred yards, not at only fifteen or twenty yards. A much greater chance of success with a smaller investment of time.

Iowa has an 'early muzzleloader season' in mid-October each year, and for various reasons, that timing worked best for my daughter. I talked to a friend who agreed to help me put up a two-person tree stand on his property so I could sit with my daughter and help her during her first-ever deer hunt. She had a new in-line muzzleloader that we had 'sighted in' and that she had practiced with enough to feel comfortable. On the opening day of the season, a Saturday, we woke up well before dawn and drove to my friend's property. The tree stand was not far from where we parked my truck, and we walked quietly through the predawn darkness to the base of the ladder leading up to the two-person seat fifteen feet off the ground. We tied her, charged, but not primed, muzzleloader to the gear haul rope, clipped ourselves to a safety rope, and climbed up to the seat. We pulled up the gun and sat down with about twenty minutes to go before the legal shooting light. I told her to go ahead and put in the primer. We jostled around a bit to get comfortable and settled in for a long wait until a deer, maybe, would come into range. It was a glorious morning. Chilly, but not cold, and a very light breeze. The yellow, orange, and red leaves of fall were glowing in the growing light. We heard a rooster pheasant crow in the distance. A red bellied woodpecker (*Melanerpes carolinus*) stopped by to see if our tree was a good spot for breakfast.

Deer are 'crepuscular', meaning that they are most active around dawn and around dusk, though they can be seen most any time of day. Legal shooting light arrived, and my daughter was 'actually deer hunting'. We had sat for about ten minutes when I glanced to my left. There was a deer, a large doe, that had in total silence shown up only a few yards from our stand. I squeezed my daughter's knee and whispered 'deer'. The doe walked right in front of us and stood broadside at about fifteen yards. My daughter whispered, 'should I shoot'? I whispered back 'take your time and shoot when you're ready'. Boom. When the spark from the primer reaches the gunpowder both the projectile and a LOT of smoke exit the muzzle of the gun. Sitting just to her left side, I saw the deer fall. My daughter, looking directly through the cloud of smoke, saw a deer, that we had not previously noticed, go bounding off through the woods to her right. She turned to me and said "@#*&...how did I miss?" I smiled, and said "you didn't." Her deer was lying dead right where she had shot it through the heart.

My daughter was noticeably shaking as she climbed down the ladder to the ground. We walked a few yards, and there laid the deer on the ground. I said, "you actually could have shot this one with a bow." My daughter knelt down and touched the deer's side. It's a powerful, and emotional, thing to see first-hand where the meat on your dinner plate comes from. It's much easier to not care at all about the animal when you buy meat wrapped in plastic at the grocery store. My son-in-law joined us and was laughing as he pointed out that he had barely gotten into the deer stand he was using before he heard the shot. I told my daughter to 'never, ever, expect any future deer hunt to turn out like this one'. We set about field dressing the deer and then dragging it back to the truck to take it home. We hung up the deer using a block and tackle, washed it out, and then skinned it and quartered it. The next day we butchered the deer, and my daughter was ready to take home meat that would feed her family for months. Meat from an animal that had lived a happy life and that she had killed herself. These days, my daughter routinely adds a deer to her family's freezer each fall.

# Ducks

*Unlike a deer, a duck can see you in color and from a very long way off… if you can see a duck, it can see you.*

Heather Carver

Similar to the relationship that Skunk River Navy student volunteers had previously had with their local streams, I had been near marshes for much of my life but had spent very little time in them. Mostly, I tried to avoid marshes because of the bugs, mud, and difficult travel. To be fair, the Iowa settlers of European descent, and their descendants, had spent well over a hundred years trying to get rid of marshes before I came on the scene. So, there weren't all that many marshes that needed to be avoided. Going duck hunting for the first time on a cloudy late November day with occasional bursts of sleet changed all that. One of my ex-students was guiding me, and he had brought duck decoys and a pair of chest waders for me.

I had eaten very little duck in my life and was yet to discover the sumptuous taste of skin-on, pan-seared, medium rare duck. Paired with honey-cinnamon roasted sweet potatoes, spinach salad, and a nice Pinot Noir it was a 'fancy dinner out' while at home. That realization was still a way off in the future. At the moment I was consumed with, essentially, a bird watching task while standing in ice water wearing borrowed chest waders. Was that a flock of ducks or a flock of red-winged black birds (*Agelaius phoeniceus*)? Were they flying toward us, or away from us? If they were ducks, were they mallards (*Anas platyrhynchos*), green-winged teal (*Anas carolinensis*), northern pintails (*Anas acuta*), or maybe some other kind of duck? Maybe they were Canada geese (*Branta canadensis*)? This was very cool, both figuratively and literally. A lone drake northern shoveler (*Spatula clypeata*) almost got close enough to shoot at and then it was gone, as was legal shooting light for the day.

I had seen bird species that I had rarely, or never, seen before. I had waded into a marsh and enjoyed it (well, not the deep sticky mud part). I had learned that one did not actually have to have a big, expensive, boat to go duck hunting. I wanted to do more duck hunting, a lot more. But first, I needed chest waders that fit, some duck decoys, duck calls, some goose decoys, a waterproof camouflaged pack, and eventually, a small, cheap, duck boat with a blind. I also had to learn how to back up a trailer. Duck hunting is quite gear intensive, but having the gear in no way guarantees success. Success is the result of lots of attempts, mostly failures, learning to make a duck call sound vaguely like a duck, scouting out places that ducks like where it's also legal to hunt ducks, learning to correctly identify ducks (and geese) to comply with various seasons and species-specific daily limits. I started duck hunting way too late in life to ever be 'good' at it. In short, waterfowl hunting is more complicated than pheasant hunting in which the most challenging question is typically 'was that a rooster or a hen that just scared the &*#@ out of me?'.

Although it is true that walking into marshes to hunt ducks, while carrying a small amount of gear, can be successful, what turns out to be most important is being flexible enough (and having the needed gear) to be able to use various approaches to get to where the ducks want to be. Sometimes, walking in is the right approach, other times a canoe is a better way to get to where you need to be. In other circumstances, a shallow draft boat with a mud motor is a better choice, either to hunt from the boat using a boat blind, or to use the boat to get to the desired location and then build a blind to hunt from somewhere outside the boat. Basically, it depends on your assessment of the circumstances, and there is no shortage of opportunities to make the wrong choice. But, however, you get there, and no matter how hard you have to work to get decoys set out and to get well hidden, once all is ready the true magic begins. The high-pitched stuttering call of a sora rail (*Porzana carolina*). A muskrat (*Ondatra zibethicus*) swimming past you before soundlessly diving below the surface of the water. A northern harrier (*Circus cyaneus*) cruising over the cattails searching for an easy meal. A raft of American coots (*Fulica americana*) all taking off at the same time while their feet churn up the water to achieve sufficient speed to become airborne. A pair of trumpeter swans (*Cygnus buccinator*) moving through the water with no discernable effort whatsoever. It's enough to make you wonder why anyone would avoid marshes. Sometimes, you even see ducks. Usually, the ducks are flying away from you, or completely ignoring your duck calls, or they start to fly toward you and then turn away well before reaching the edge of shotgun range. But not always.

Duck hunting is one of the more social forms of hunting because you're often sitting close to a hunting buddy, you're not out-of-breath from walking uphill through thick grassy cover, the majority of the time the sky is duck-free, and there's no need to be quiet unless there are ducks very close. Plenty of time for discussing whatever happens to be on your collective minds. On one duck hunting trip a friend and I took my boat, a 14-foot-long flat bottom boat with a small 'long-tail' mud motor, to the upstream reaches of a large reservoir. It was a sunny, chilly, late season day but there was no ice on the water. We parked the boat along the muddy bank of a narrow channel and hauled decoys and other gear through a couple hundred yards of muddy ground, covered mostly with 'cocklebur' (*Xanthium strumarium*), to reach a landlocked pond.

Cocklebur produces fruits with hooked projections that stick to clothing (and fur) very well. They are not as annoying as the fruits of 'burdock' (*Arctium minus*), in my opinion, but they still aren't much fun to pick off of your dog. Burdock is also not a 'native' species. It was introduced (unintentionally) from Europe. Lest you think that only non-native species are annoying, one interaction with 'round-leaf greenbrier' (*Smilax rotiundifolia*), which is native, and its numerous, needle sharp, black spines will convince you otherwise.

We built blinds near the edge of the pond to hide from sharp-eyed ducks using willows (members of genus *Salix*) and many armfuls of sedges (members of genus *Carex*). There were lots of ducks around and we had a good day, shooting our limits by early afternoon. We hadn't been paying careful attention, but it was clear that it had become significantly windier as the day had progressed. Most of our return trip was on narrow winding channels, but the last half mile or so to the boat ramp was a larger open bay. As we emerged from a channel into the open bay, we could see white caps on the water. It seemed a little 'sketchy', but we thought we would be alright. Just to be sure, I first guided the boat at an angle across the bay to be near the shoreline that my truck was parked on. Then we turned into the wind and headed for the boat ramp. There was quite a lot of spray coming over the bow at times. We almost made it. About twenty-five yards from the boat ramp a larger wave came over the bow and the boat filled with water. My dog was the first to abandon ship, presumably figuring that she was in a boat with idiots. We were lucky. We were near shore, and the water was only waist deep. We gathered our gear as it was floating out of the boat and threw it onto shore. Then we waded with the boat to the ramp, backed the trailer into the water, winched the boat onto the trailer, used the truck to pull the boat out of the water, opened the drain plug, and waited for the boat to empty. It was a good reminder of the inherent dangers of being out in nature. It was also quite clear that a small, overloaded, boat with little free board was not a good idea in windy conditions. Better to wait for conditions to improve.

Always keeping the dangers in mind, there's plenty of times that I find myself hunting ducks on my own. On a recent outing, I was at a local cattail marsh that has two rudimentary boat ramps. I had accessed the marsh from one of the ramps several times, so I thought it might be a good day to try the other access. Exploration can lead to rewards. The boat ramp and the channel leading through the cattails toward the open water I intended to hunt looked quite reasonable. I loaded all the decoys and other gear into the boat and backed the trailer into the water. It was a sunny and breezy day, but it was sheltered in the cattails. I parked my truck and launched my boat. At first, all went well. The boat was moving quickly through a narrow, winding, channel in the cattails. It seemed clear that other boats had passed this way in the recent past, and most duck boats are bigger than mine. The first sign of trouble was the boat lurching, and slowing down, as it hit the muddy bottom repeatedly. But this is what shallow draft boats with mud motors are for – moving through shallow water. I kept going, slowly, but going. The boat came around a sharper bend, the water seemed deeper, and then, the boat came to a complete stop. The bow of the boat was tightly wedged between two very stout muskrat houses. The structural integrity of cattails and mud blended together is quite remarkable. Long-tail motors do not have reverse, only forward, and no amount of revving the motor was moving the boat forward. Pushing as hard as I could with my long duck-billed 'push-pole' was ineffective at moving the boat backward. I was left with the only option being to get out of the boat, always a 'crap shoot' in a cattail marsh and seeing whether I could push the boat backward. The water HAD gotten deeper, and when combined with the soft mud on the bottom, the water was up past my waist. After a considerable amount of pushing, while having quite poor leverage, and numerous 'choice words', the boat started moving backward.

My problems, however, were not over, it was a long, muddy, wade back to the boat ramp that I was not wanting to undertake, the motor had no reverse, and making things more interesting was that the channel in the cattails was far too narrow to turn the boat around. I had to get out to the open water. It was at this point I noted that at least one person had gotten a boat through here. They had passed through a thinner spot in the cattails to the left of the muskrat houses. It wasn't easy, wading through the mud and towing the boat, but I got my boat through and made it to the open water. I could have set up to hunt then and there, but I had no desire to pass through this narrow channel in the dark at the end of the day. I turned the boat around, made it past the muskrat houses again, and motored back to the ramp. That was the last time I'll be using that boat ramp. Exploration does not always lead to rewards, but sometimes it tells you what not to do.

After putting the boat back on the trailer, I drove around to the other boat ramp and re-launched my boat. I was sweaty, tired, and more than a little aggravated. I motored to a small, shallower, bay and hid the boat in the cattails. The wind was right at my back, meaning that any ducks wanting to land would be coming right toward me. I waded around setting up decoys and, finally, crawled back into the boat to actually start hunting. There were a few ducks flying around, but not many. One hen mallard landed well out of range and paddled lazily around, taunting me. Then I heard wings flying downwind right overhead and looked up to see a pair of mallards turning upwind and flying right toward me. Their wings locked up and their orange feet were hanging beneath them. I shot the drake, and my dog leaped out of the boat to swim over and retrieve it. Watching your dog swim back with a duck in her mouth never gets old. Any hunt during which you get a duck is a good one, but I was, of course, hoping for more. We didn't see any more ducks. But we did see something better. A pair of white-faced ibises (*Plegadis chihi*), which are definitely not legal to bring home for dinner, showed up very unexpectedly. They flew around the little bay, repeatedly landing on muskrat houses and mats of floating cattails. I got a great look at them and their dark-colored iridescent feathers. I had never seen a white-faced ibis before and had to do some 'research' when I got home to be able to put a name to what I had seen. These birds breed primarily west of Iowa and overwinter in Mexico. They only rarely fly through Iowa during the fall migration. I was very fortunate to have seen them. No matter how much you've seen of the natural world, there's always more to see and more to learn.

# What's in Your Nature?

*The first rule of intelligent tinkering is to save all the parts.*

Paul R. Ehrlich

Thankfully, not everyone is born to be a winter camper, or a biologist. Successful human societies require people with a wide range of interests and skills. Carpenters, medical personnel, engineers, cooks, map makers, wait staff, factory workers, researchers, farmers, baristas, truck drivers, teachers, artists, bankers, musicians, architects, therapists, road construction workers, political leaders, and a much, much, longer list. We each try to identify the interests, abilities, and skills that we possess, and that will allow us to contribute. At most, we each do the best we can, and, without a doubt, each of us will fail in some of our aspirations. It's very difficult for any one person to know precisely how much their contributions may have led to the success (or failure) of their society. Did a surgeon who saved the lives of one hundred people contribute less than a surgeon who saved the lives of one thousand people? What if one of those hundred people went on to do research that dramatically improved the lives of millions of people? What if one of the thousand people went on to become a political leader who ushered in policies leading to a dramatic decrease in the quality of life for most members of their society? The contribution of any one person, or even a category of people with a common set of skills, to the success of a society, may well be impossible to assess. The success, or failure, of any system depends on contributions from various, often numerous, parts. If enough parts are lost, the system will fail, and it is never clear just how many parts can 'safely' be lost.

Natural ecosystems can be thought of in a similar way. This does not imply that 'humans' or 'human societies' are not natural – they most certainly are. But we can extend the idea of individual humans contributing to their societies, to thinking in terms of individual species contributing to their ecosystems. Some contributions are rather obvious. Every photosynthetic plant species contributes, at a minimum, by producing 'food' through the process of photosynthesis, and also by producing oxygen along the way. But not all plants are photosynthetic. Members of the flowering plant species called 'ghost plant' (*Monotropa uniflora*) do not carry out photosynthesis. They are, as you might expect from their name, a ghostly white in color. They obtain their food via a relationship with a fungus, which, in turn, is in a mycorrhizal relationship with a photosynthetic plant. This is called being a 'mycoheterotroph'. We know what a ghost plant is NOT contributing to its ecosystem, but that does not lead to the conclusion: 'they aren't contributing anything – and are, therefore, unimportant'. A much more accurate conclusion is that 'we don't know what they are contributing'. This is in no way surprising because the natural world is very complex and there is a great deal we don't understand.

A similar comment can be made about most of the, literally, millions of species we currently share the Earth with. Many of these species, especially the smaller ones, we've not even 'met', i.e., assigned them names, let alone begun to understand what contributions they make to their ecosystems. Even the ecosystem contributions of well-known species are often poorly, or incompletely, understood. We know, for example, that predators kill their prey species, but what other ecosystem contributions may the predators be making?

Minimizing the spread of infectious diseases amongst members of the prey species? Maximizing the productivity of plant species in the ecosystem by decreasing herbivory? Often, we simply don't know the answers to such questions.

> *The last word in ignorance is the man who says of an animal or plant: "What good is it?"*
>
> Aldo Leopold

In my role as a biology teacher, I was often asked by students, after they learned of the existence of some new (to them) species, 'well – what is the purpose of that species?'. This, of course, is a very 'human-centric' perspective. What they are really asking is 'can humans eat this species, use this species as a source of medicines, or, more broadly, derive economic benefit from this species?'. The implication being that, if humans cannot make some use of the species, it has 'no purpose'. The reality is that all species have the 'purpose' of reproducing to make more of their species, and that all species contribute in some way (whether we know how, or not) to their ecosystems. The huge impacts of human population and technology have led to the extinction (global loss), extirpation (local loss), and diminution of populations of many species. Some of the affected species we may never even have realized existed – we'd not 'met' and named them. In essence, due to our activities, we're 'throwing away' parts of ecosystems without knowing what contributions they make.

Human activities have diminished, or eliminated, various ecosystems around the globe. The tallgrass prairie ecosystem of Iowa (and nearby states) has been almost entirely replaced in favor of row crop agriculture. The populations of many tallgrass species have dramatically decreased. Some species have been extirpated (e.g., elk; *Cervus canadensis*). We know very little about particular species that may have been pushed to extinction because we have an incomplete list of the species that were present before the conversion from tallgrass prairie to cropland. We've not yet impacted the Earth's ecosystems to the extent that humans are no longer able to survive. The 'bad news' is that we still might, and that we would likely take with us into the abyss of extinction many more of the species that currently live on Earth. The 'good news' is that humans, even with all of our technology, lack the power to extinguish all life on Earth. No matter how dramatically we alter the current ecosystems, some species will be 'ok with that' and will continue on reproducing and contributing to whatever ecosystems they are part of. As long stretches of time pass, these species, through the never-ending process of evolution, will produce a huge diversity of species that are parts of various ecosystems around the planet. From a human perspective this is a very small consolation.

If we would rather not push even more species, possibly including our own, to extinction, many more people will have to care about biological diversity. The more people who care, the more likely that the political will, and financial resources, needed to protect and preserve our current biological diversity, can be marshalled to achieve that outcome. This is a major challenge that has many aspects, but one fundamental aspect is that it's impossible to care about something that you don't know exists. So, one part of the solution is to increase the number of people who know more of the amazing organisms that we share this planet with. People in Iowa, for example, are quite familiar with corn, soybeans, alfalfa, cattle, pigs, and chickens, but not many are familiar with 'yellow-rumped warblers' (*Setophaga coronata*) that migrate through Iowa each fall and spring, or with 'northern hogsuckers' (*Hypentelium nigricans*) fish that live in the less polluted of our streams. There is a long list of additional Iowa species that not many Iowans are familiar with.

There are many approaches for learning of the existence of the various species we share our world with. Knowledgeable mentors, including family and friends, can be very useful. We should be very appreciative of any mentors we have and strive to become mentors ourselves. Books on the diversity within various groups of organisms can be helpful. For those with access, college-level classes on biological diversity can provide in-depth exposure and understanding. Nature documentaries can be important, especially about places far from where you live. But what I want to emphasize is the importance of 'knowing your neighbors', the biodiversity in your 'backyard', even inside your house, e.g., the 'house centipede' (*Scutigera coleoptrata*) or the 'box elder bug' (*Boisea trivittata*). If we don't understand the amazing diversity in our local environment, it's easy to conclude that biodiversity is mostly present somewhere far away that you can only see on a nature documentary, and there's not much you can do about protecting it. Spending most of a lifetime figuring such things out, as I have, is not realistic for the vast majority of people. Fortunately, there are amazing new technologies that can help us meet the neighbors. One of the easiest to use is 'iNaturalist'. This is a free app that one can download to their smartphone. You simply register, take a picture of some organism (or part of an organism, e.g., a feather), and share the picture. Within a short period of time, you're likely to have a response, from someone more knowledgeable, providing the name of the organism you were curious about. I highly recommend walking around in a natural area with a young person and taking pictures of flowers, bugs, and birds, and whatever organisms you see to ask iNaturalist about.

> *Unless someone like you cares a whole awful lot, nothing is going to get better. It's not.*
>
> Dr. Seuss

Hopefully, people who are more aware of the biodiversity that they are surrounded by, will care more about protecting biodiversity. Knowing, and caring, about biological diversity can, actually, have beneficial effects. Consider the 'trumpeter swan' (*Cygnus buccinator*). Trumpeter swans were found in abundance throughout the state of Iowa when people of European heritage began to settle in the area in the early 1800s. By 1883, due to unregulated hunting and draining of wetlands for agriculture, these majestic birds were extirpated from Iowa. By 1932 there were only sixty-nine trumpeter swans remaining in the entire United States. But enough people knew about, and cared about, trumpeter swans. They were protected and their populations began to recover. In 1993 efforts to reintroduce trumpeter swans into Iowa were initiated. By 2020, there were over one hundred nesting pairs of trumpeter swans in Iowa. I have been fortunate enough to closely observe trumpeter swans while duck hunting on numerous occasions. Knowing, and caring, about biological diversity can work.

In the modern world, many of us think that we live apart from nature. That we are, somehow, above and beyond the natural world. Nothing, of course, could be further from the truth. The food we eat, regardless of how indirect our connection to it is, is all from the natural world. The oxygen in the air we breathe is produced by the natural world; plants on land and 'phytoplankton' in water. The medicines we use are often derived directly from the natural world or have been inspired by the natural world. We suffer from infectious diseases that are part of the natural world. When we die, our atoms will (eventually) become some other part of the natural world. Other than being shot into space on a one-way trip, there is no escaping the natural world here on Earth. We are inherently, and completely, part of the natural world, even if we can sit comfortably in a heated home on a cold winter day and look at a smartphone.

I have often wondered how our ancient ancestors learned what species in their local environment were dangerous and what species were good for dinner. Did they just pick different kinds of mushrooms, try them, and then keep eating the ones that nobody in their group died from? How did they figure out what species of snakes were venomous and which ones were 'nothing to worry about', and probably good for dinner? What was the approach for determining which species of plants had medicinal properties and which caused severe contact dermatitis? All of these are much 'higher stakes' forms of learning about biological diversity than is iNaturalist. They had to have been exquisitely careful observers of the biodiversity present around them. And, without any 'peer-reviewed scientific literature' to consult, they had to be good at telling stories that effectively communicated to the next generation what mushrooms, snakes, and plants should definitely be avoided. It has long been in the nature of our species to closely observe the biological world we live in, and to communicate those observations to others.

My hope in telling my stories is to help inspire others to become 'careful observers' of the world they live in. To notice not only the larger, more charismatic creatures, but also come to know something about the myriad smaller, and less obvious, organisms we share this world with. And then, generously, share that knowledge with others, both young and old. Doing so is in your nature.

> *In the end we will conserve only what we love; we will love only what we understand; and we will understand only what we are taught.*
>
> Baba Dioum

# Acknowledgments

I thank my parents, Jim and Nancy, for providing early experiences in the natural world and always encouraging learning. My siblings, Susan, Sally, Mary, and Marty, deserve many thanks for following me around on early adventures, even when they probably shouldn't have. All my science teachers (especially biology) played a crucial role in developing my perspective on the world. Thanks to all my biology students who may have helped me learn more than I helped them learn. And finally, a big thank you to my wife, Karen, who helped edit this book (though all mistakes, of course, are mine) and has supported me and put up with my, sometimes sketchy, ideas for the past fifty years.

www.ingramcontent.com/pod-product-compliance
Lightning Source LLC
Chambersburg PA
CBHW061749070526
44585CB00025B/2841